D1261268

THE GIFT OF THE RIVER

By the Author

THE GIFT OF THE RIVER

BY WAGON AND FLATBOAT

ABRAHAM LINCOLN

SILVER FOR GENERAL WASHINGTON

THE FIRST YEAR

ON INDIAN TRAILS WITH DANIEL BOONE

BY SECRET RAILWAY

TEXAS STAR

HOLDING THE FORT WITH DANIEL BOONE

THE GIFT OF THE RIVER

A History of Ancient Egypt

BY

Enid LaMonte Meadowcroft

Introduction by Kirk Meadowcroft

Illustrations adapted from Egyptian sources by
KATHARINE DEWEY

THOMAS Y. CROWELL COMPANY
PUBLISHERS - - - NEW YORK

Fourteenth Printing

PRINTED IN THE UNITED STATES OF AMERICA

To

Clara P. Meadowcroft

Table of Contents

TO THE CHILDREN

You have read about the cave-men and remember that they were called pre-historic because they lived before history was written. You know how they learned about fire, how they shaped their weapons and guarded the homes that they took from the wild animals. You know how they learned to grow their food and to tame some of those animals, how they lived together and learned to govern themselves, how they took the first steps toward building what we call Civilization.

In this book I have tried to tell you the story of the first people we know of who were really civilized—the first people to write history. They lived thousands of years ago in a land quite different from our own—yet we owe to them many things which make up our daily lives. As you read this story you will find that these people had strange and curious customs. But if you read it thoughtfully you will find that many of their customs are no more strange and curious than our own. You will find that men who lived thousands of years ago were not so different from men who live today.

I hope you will like the book. If you do, you as well as I must be grateful to those people who have helped to make it.

E. L. M.

FOR GROWN-UPS

History may be counted as among the subjects dearest to the heart of man. In many periods of his existence, history, out of the nature of its presentation, has changed; in part altered to conform with the changing culture of the age in which it was written—in part estranged to us by the inevitable alteration of words and their meanings. But in the last analysis, whether the age has led men to study it as a guide to a successful life, as a determinative source of a human ethic, or as a source of human knowledge, it remains to us the last mirror of human conduct. In the exaltation of each hope, in the despairing recapitulation of each failure, man has turned to a studied contemplation of the past.

So, more than all, history must come to us cleanly, free from scholastic prejudgment, free from ethical bias, free from personal animus. Yet great events, like great mountains, can best be measured by distant survey, and the results checked by the general laws applying to each. Egypt, despite the disorganization of its material for study, and the ease with which that material has been often misinterpreted in the past, offers us at least this long perspective into time. We can check the basic facts that concern the existence of the Egyptians as a people and their nature as human beings, on the one hand, by those remotest burials of unnamed races that lived scattered over the earth in the very dawn of man, and on the other, by the behavior of races known to us, in well-documented periods.

The whole spirit and teaching of history have changed very radically in the space of a comparatively short period of years. It is no longer accepted or rejected merely from its conformity to certain conventional beliefs, nor taught as a series of events upon which sermons and morals may be based.

The history of Greece and Rome has been

in our day swept clear of the golden haze of legend that threatened it as fatally as the miasma that choked out their ancient cities. And with this clearer view of the past, we are no longer able to accept either of these great cultures as original with those races alone. We find them no less great for having learned from elder peoples some of the wisdom and beauty that they developed by their own genius.

In our own cultural heritage of thought, of worship and of speech itself, we can recognize many germs, now covered over and disguised by the accretions of alien centuries, that they and no others sent down the future to our time.

And the histories of Greece and Rome are seen no longer as the stories of little tribal groups, founding upstart settlements and flowering, for no apparent reason, into great empires of superlative arts, but rather as passing whirlpools in a great cultural stream—vortices that drew into their center for a time all the drifting cargo of the current, only to scatter it again free upon the surface.

Until at last we see that time and men's thoughts go on endlessly—only the names are changed. Yesterday might be Today; and Tomorrow is their twin-brother. We are all pawns in the hand of Time.

KIRK MEADOWCROFT

I

THE GIFT OF THE RIVER

In far-off Africa flows the great River Nile. It is a strange river, unlike almost all others in the world. Rising in central and eastern Africa, it flows north for nearly four thousand miles. Sometimes it goes through rocky country, sometimes through sandy desert hills, twisting and turning in its effort to reach the ocean. Where the river has been unable to cut its way through the rocks, it swirls and dashes in foaming cataracts. There are six of these cataracts in its course. But when the Nile is almost a hundred miles from the sea it has become a wide river that divides into separate streams and flows on until it pours its waters into the Mediterranean Sea. As its current becomes slower and slower, it lets fall the rich earth that it has carried from far up the Sudan. During thousands of years this earth has built new land, through which the river flows in different channels. Once, long, long ago, there were seven of these smaller streams. Today there are only two. Because the land through which these small rivers pass is the shape of the Greek letter Δ it is called the Delta.

The Nile is a most convenient and in many ways, a most friendly river. Our own Mississippi goes calmly on its way day after day, and then, fed by unusual rains or by melting snows, it overflows its banks, floods the surrounding country, ruins homes and does much damage. The Nile overflows, too—but it does it regularly, calmly, almost as though it were blessing the land that it floods. It does indeed bless the land, for when the waters recede they leave behind them rich layers of the black, fertile mud that has been carried down from Central Africa. For miles inland, on either side of the stream, it brings new life to growing things and new things begin to grow.

It is on the banks of the river, in a land known to us as Egypt, that men first began to make what we call History.

When we study the history of Egypt, it is very much as if we were to find ourselves in a deserted playroom, where toys lie about in heaps, scattered and broken. And it is from a study of these toys that we must try to discover what the children were like who used them, who they were, how they lived, and what they liked best to play. The toys have gathered dust for thousands of years, and the playroom is very dark. But slowly, as our eyes become accustomed to the darkness, we can make out places where generations of those children have written their names upon the playroom walls. And as we sort out the heaps of broken toys we find, at the very bottom, things that belonged to children who lived so long ago that they didn't know how to write their names at all.

How can we find out who those children were, and what they did?

In Egypt for many years skilled men have been digging steadily, under the hot Egyptian sun, hoping to unearth all sorts of buried treasure, knowing that wonderful things have already been found under the rocks and sand. They are digging, not because of any wealth they may gain for themselves, but in the hope of finding something which will help us to learn more about the names, lives and thoughts of those first men who made history along the Nile.

You see, those Egyptian people, who lived there thousands of years ago, believed that life on this earth was only a preparation—a getting-ready—for a much longer and more peaceful life in another world. Homes that they built on this earth they called "inns for travelers"; but the tomb that was built for a man who had died they called "house of everlasting."

One of the first things that an Egyptian did when he became a man was to plan and begin to build his tomb. He wanted a tomb that was beautiful and so strongly built that it would last forever. Then when he died, in order that

A WOMAN MOURNS BEFORE A MUMMY CASE WHICH CONTAINS THE BODY OF A MAN WHO HAS DIED

his body might last him well on his journey to the next world, and in his next life, it was embalmed. That means it was treated with oils and spices, and carefully wrapped in strips of linen cloth. Then it was placed in a wooden case and the case put in the tomb. And buried with his body were many of the things that the man had used and loved, for the journey to the next world must be made comfortably, and once there he must have the things he might need to live happily.

All men were alike in their thought of death, and even when a man became King he, too, took first thought for the building of his "house of everlasting," planning it carefully. Many men worked on it for years, bringing the stone they needed from across the River Nile, or the highly-prized red granite from away up the river. And of course when the king was buried, gorgeous things were buried with him—jewels and fine linens, vases of alabaster, statues of gold and of ebony, furniture inlaid with ivory, bows and arrows and spears, even his chariots, walking sticks and gloves. On the walls of his tomb were painted pictures and writings which told of the things that had happened during his life.

These buried treasures are the things for which men are still digging in Egypt. They are valuable to own and beautiful to look upon; but they are much more than that. They show us who are living thousands of years later, how these far-away people lived, what they wore, where they traveled, what they ate, and even what they thought. And, strangely enough, the more we study the things which these men discover, the more we find that those ancient people were very, very like ourselves.

However, their language has long since been forgotten, and the meanings of the writings on the walls of their tombs might have been lost to us forever, had there not been a fortunate discovery.

About a hundred and thirty years ago, the famous French general, Napoleon, led an army into Egypt. Soldiers were digging a trench not far from Rosetta, a town near the mouth of the Nile. Suddenly one man's pick struck a stone, which with great effort he dug up. As he was about to heave it to one side, he noticed that it was covered with strange markings, evidently some sort of writing, and though he had no idea what it might mean, he studied it with care.

The stone was black, a little over two feet wide, and almost four feet long. Three of the corners had broken off or crumbled away. It was divided into three sections and each section bore a different kind of marking.

The soldier was curious about it. He cleaned it off carefully and showed it to his superior officer. When the army returned to France they took the stone with them. Later it was sent to England and placed in the British Museum. It is called the Rosetta Stone and it was this stone that helped men to learn to read the old Egyptian language. Its three sections were each in a different language but all told the same story; so it furnished a "key."

At the top was the very old Egyptian picture writing called hieroglyphics. In the middle was the writing used by the Egyptians later on, called hieratic. The bottom section was Greek.

No one in all the world, not even in Egypt, could read either of the old Egyptian languages, but there were scholars who could read Greek. Still it was not easy. Only after years of study, did the funny little pictures and queer marks on the stone begin to mean something to the students who were working over them. But at last men of our own time were able to tell what some of the writing on the walls of the tombs says, and to read some of the old Egyptian books.

And so to the men who dig in the sand and the rocks; to the soldier who was curious; and to scholars who have spent years in studying the writing, we should be grateful. For they have helped us to go back thousands of years and to become acquainted with the men and women, the boys and girls, who made their homes on the River Nile.

II

THE SHADOW PEOPLE

(Time, Over 6000 Years Ago)

Who were these people who lived in Egypt so long ago? Where did they come from?

The first men who lived in the Nile valley were wandering tribes of hunters. We know nothing of them, except what has been learned from a few tools and weapons of crudely chipped flint, which have been dug up or found in their graves. These tools are exactly like those made by early men in other parts of the world.

Then some people we call Libyans or Lebu (we don't know what they called themselves) settled along the river. They had been living on the north coast of Africa on the shores of the great Libyan Sea. This sea occupied then the place where much of the Sahara Desert is now. For a long time the climate of the country had been changing. The rains, which had been coming less and less often, grew so scarce that the new leaves withered and the forest died. There had been rumblings and earthquakes. Then with a great final tremor and roaring the whole eastern edge of Africa, that for centuries and centuries had been pushed higher and higher by the tremendous forces under the earth, suddenly reached the limit of its strength and collapsed. And those men, who lived on the shores of the sea, may have seen the water suddenly flow northward and disappear, carrying with it their tribesmen and their belongings.

Of course, dreadful times followed for those who were left. There were floods and famine, and the tribes of Libya had to find new homes and food. Those who were lucky found caves where they could shelter themselves from the burning heat of the sun. But the plants all dried up and the game animals grew scarcer and scarcer, until finally there were no more. Then they lived on the snails that ate the scant grass that grew around their caves.

At last one of them must have wandered farther away than the others, in his search for food—wandered until he came to the Nile, which carried the water that meant life. Think of his joy as he hurried back to tell his friends! Many of them followed him and made their homes along the new-found river.

Hundreds of years after the Libyans had settled on the Nile, a new race of people crossed into Egypt from some place along the Red Sea. They seem to have been tall and strong and though there were not so many of them, so that they could not have conquered the owners of the land by fighting, yet in a little while they became the kings and nobles of Upper Egypt.

For some hundreds of years all of these people lived along the Nile in their little villages. And through the years, the men of the villages fought with one another about many things, but perhaps chiefly about land. Fertile ground was scarce. When one village wanted more land on which to grow its food, there was only one thing to do—take it away from some weaker town. And so they fought, one village joining with another to fight its neighbor, until at last they banded themselves together into two great kingdoms, Lower Egypt and Upper Egypt.

The ruler of Lower Egypt was called the Bee king. He wore a bright red crown and in the titles of all the Bee kings we find a picture of a bee. The king of Upper Egypt was called the Reed king. His crown was white, and there is always the sign of the reed in his titles.

We know very little of those early rulers. They have left us no tombs, no pyramids, and no records. At most we have only a few empty graves, paved with brick and fenced with wood, and one or two objects, such as a great mace which belonged to the Scorpion King and a palette belonging to a king called Narmer. These men moved like shadows through the earliest part of the story of Egypt.

But though we know so little of the actual

lives and names of these first kings, we know much more of what was done by their people. For a king may die and his name be forgotten, but the things he teaches his people are the foundation on which the next people must build, and these are not entirely forgotten. And at a time when men in most other parts of the world had not yet learned even how to live peacefully together, the Egyptians had discovered many important things.

Each year when the sun had burned the land until it was dry and parched, the waters of the Nile would begin to rise and would continue rising for many days. With what joy men saw their fields flooded; knowing that when the waters receded fresh crops would grow quickly, and that once more their country would be green. But often in those early years the waters would do great damage; so in order to protect themselves, men learned to build their villages on artificial hills and to erect dikes between the river and their farms.

The wise men of the court also studied the river, on which all their lives depended, and learned when to expect it to overflow. They marked on rocks the rise and fall of the water, and after some years of study they were able to tell the people when and where it was best to plant their crops.

As it rains seldom in that part of Africa, men had to find some way of watering their fields in the season when the Nile was low. Wherever possible they dug ditches and little canals that would carry the water from the Nile into fields near by. Then some man, more thoughtful than his neighbor, realized that if the water could be carried to the hills beyond the fertile land, they too would yield good harvests. So at the ends of his canals which led from the Nile he dug a series of wells in rows, one row above another, almost as we build our terraces. Then he cut ditches leading from the last row of wells to the new fields he wished to water. In order to get the water from the lower wells to the higher ones he used a *shaduf*—an upright pole with a beam slung across it. On one end of the beam he hung a bucket for raising water, and on the other he fastened a large lump of mud, which helped to raise and balance the bucket.

Soon there were in Egypt many people whose daily work was to draw the water from the lower wells and to empty it into those higher, until at last it reached the terraces that would otherwise have been barren. This was the first method of irrigation of which we know.

Farmers the world over must watch the sun and the moon and the clouds, in order to know when to plant and harvest their crops. So these early people, after centuries of study of the stars, the sun, the moon, the seasons and the rising of the Nile, made themselves a calendar.

They divided the year into three seasons of four months each. The first season was marked by the rise, overflow and fall of the Nile. The second was the season of planting and the third, the season of harvesting. In each month there were thirty days, and the five days that were left were used as sacred days. It is this calendar, changed slightly hundreds of years later by the Romans, that we use today.

WATERING THE FIELDS BY MEANS OF A SHADUF

No one can watch the sun and moon travel across the sky, and the stars come and go, without wondering what they are and what moves them. So these Egyptians, like all other people in the world, wondered. The wise men of the villages thought and talked about these questions. Some were sure that the sun was a god —a power—that caused all other things to move. Perhaps the moon and the good river were gods, too. The wise men told the more simple folk their thoughts, and made up stories about these gods. They told the stories so often that soon everyone believed they were true. And they made pictures of the gods, carved their figures in wood, and molded them in clay. Of course, each man saw a different picture in his mind, and the gods took strange shapes. Usually the body was that of a man or woman, but the head was often that of an animal or bird. And in different parts of Egypt the same god was given many different forms. So in one place the goddess of the sky had the head of a cow, in another the head of a cat, and in still another the head of a lioness.

The early Egyptians believed that, like man, each god must have his own dwelling place. So they built temples. These were simple buildings at first, of mud and woven wattle. Later, people brought to the temples their offerings of food, drink and fine clothing. And because they often found it difficult to put their thoughts into words when they prayed, they got their wise men to do it for them. In this way there grew up a class of men called priests, who spent their lives apart from the people, serving in the temples.

Men who are wise enough to make themselves a calendar, and to keep records, must have some form of writing. And those early men kept their records first by means of pictures. In the beginning they drew real pictures of all the important events that they wished to record. But this took too long and was too difficult, so they stopped making elaborate pictures and drew them only in outline. Those outline pictures stood at first for complete words. For example:

was the sun

was the moon

was light

was water

was rain or storm

was a mouth

Later these same pictures stood for parts of words, or syllables. And finally the Egyptians worked out an alphabet of twenty-four consonants. They had few signs for the vowels, and very often left them out altogether. So that there should be no mistake in the meaning of a word, they put at the end of each, a sign called a determinative. Take, for instance, the word which means "night"—"qerhu." (We must put in a vowel or we could not pronounce it. As we don't know what vowels the Egyptians used in their words, we shall never know what their language sounded like when it was spoken.)

Qerhu, or night, is written so—

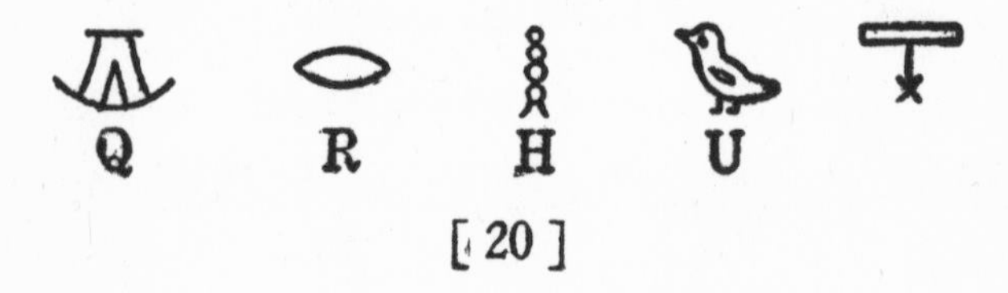

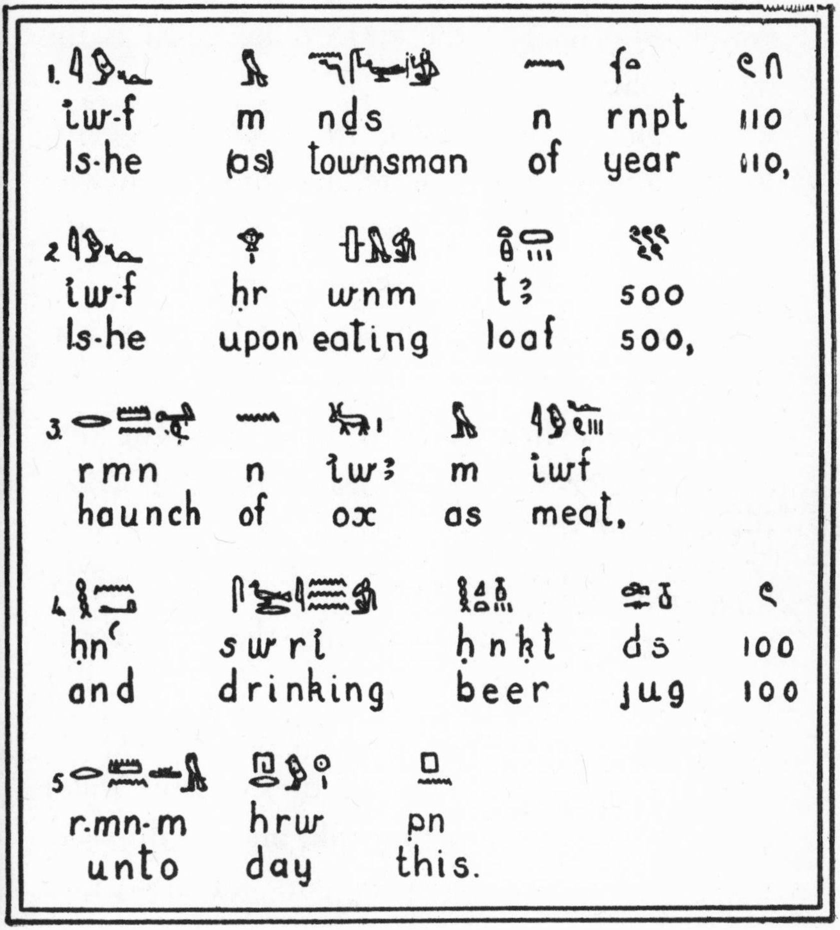

1. ỉw-f m nḏs n rnpt 110
Is-he (as) townsman of year 110,

2. ỉw-f ḥr wnm tꜣ 500
Is-he upon eating loaf 500,

3. rmn n ỉwꜣ m ỉwf
haunch of ox as meat.

4. ḥnʿ swrỉ ḥnḳt ds 100
and drinking beer jug 100

5. r-mn-m hrw pn
unto day this.

EGYPTIAN HIEROGLYPHIC WRITING
Translated freely it reads, "He is a townsman one hundred and ten years old. He eats five hundred loaves and the haunch of an ox in the way of meat and drinks a hundred jugs of beer unto this day"

The picture of the star hanging from the sky, which is placed at the end of the word is the determinative.

As the years passed, the records became longer and more elaborate, and those men who did the writing—the scribes—simplified the pictures and often ran them together. In this way the writing, which we call hieratic, was developed.

The very first early writing was cut into stone. Later some one discovered that when the stem of the papyrus plant, which grew in the marshes by the river, was stripped of its outer layer and sliced very thin, the strips could be laid together, pressed and dried. Once they were dried, they made an excellent surface on which to write. A mixture of soot and water made a strong and lasting ink, and a thin reed, sharpened or bruised at the end, was used as a pen.

So it was that at a time when our ancestors were roaming over Europe, clad in skins, killing their food where they found it, and living in caves, the Egyptians were irrigating their fields, planning in advance for their crops, building their temples, making calendars, and keeping their records.

THESE ANIMAL PICTURES WERE FOUND ON A VERY OLD FLINT KNIFE

III

THE LAND IS UNITED

(Time, About 3400–2900 B.C.)

The first Egyptian king, or Pharaoh, of which we know anything definite, was Menes the Fighter. He was about fifteen years old when he came to the throne of Upper Egypt. In spite of his youth he ruled his kingdom wisely. When he had put the affairs of his own kingdom in order he left his capital, Thinis, and marched down the Nile to Lower Egypt. Here he conquered the country and married one of the princesses with great ceremony, just like one of the old fairy tale heroes. Thus he became king of all Egypt, wearing both the white crown of the South and the red crown of the North; calling himself "Lord of the Vulture and Cobra." (The vulture represented the goddess of the southern capital city, and the cobra the goddess of the northern.)

For such a great king there must, of course, be a new capital—midway between Lower and Upper Egypt. And so, just a little way back from the Nile, among the green fields and in the path of the "sweet northern breeze," a new city grew up. It was a pleasant city where the sun shone almost always, and yet it was not too hot in summer.

The houses of the nobles usually were built around a court, in the midst of which was a pool of cool water surrounded by trees. They were made of brick, for the Egyptians had early discovered that mud from the Nile mixed with sand and a little chopped grass or straw, and shaped and dried for a couple of days in the sun, made excellent building material. The doors and gaily-decorated columns which held up the roofing beams were of wood. There were many latticed windows on all sides, which could be closed against wind or sand storms by dropping brilliantly-colored hangings.

Inside the finer houses heavy rugs covered the hard mud floors. The furniture was more beautiful than that which we use. Each piece of furniture, each jar or vase, was made by hand. Love of the work and pride in the workmanship went into the carving and decorating. Our furniture today is turned out by factories—put together by people who neither know nor care what happens to it after it has left their hands. But in Menes' time, the chests were inlaid with ivory or mica, the chairs and beds were elaborately carved, and the jars of alabaster ground so thin that the light shone through them dimly, giving them a lovely milky luster. Beauty was everywhere.

The houses of the common people varied, of course, in size and comfort, as ours do today. And those of the workmen were often only mud huts, packed so closely together that there was barely room to walk between them.

Menes ruled long in his new city, which was called Men-nofre. Later the Greeks called it Memphis. Often he appeared before his people wearing his double crown. And fastened to the back side of a short skirt made of fine white linen, which was his only garment, he wore a lion's tail. Before him walked his standard-bearers and his servants. His scribes and his fan-bearers followed in procession.

He was a strong king and a mighty hunter. With his bow and arrow or his spears, he chased the elephants, lions, giraffes, wild oxen and hippopotami, which roamed the borders of the land and came into the fields at night in order to devour the crops. Once in a hunt he chased an animal far over the desert to the edge of a lake. He traveled so far and so fast that he left his servants away behind. Suddenly his dogs—half-wild, not trained as ours are today—turned on him with savage snarls. Menes had to choose quickly between the raging dogs and the jaws of the crocodiles who lived in the lake. He plunged into the water and managed somehow to escape the hungry crocodiles. For this he was so grateful that he later built a beautiful city on the shores of that lake.

In another hunt, however, he was not so fortunate, for he died, they say, from wounds received from a hippopotamus. We know little of this great king who reigned more than five thousand years ago—only that he was so powerful that he succeeded in uniting Egypt, and that under his rule his people prospered. But though he has been so long dead, things which he used and which were used by his family are left for us to see. One of these is a beautifully worked bar of gold with his name upon it. And there are ivory toilet pieces left by his queen, some of which bear the name of his little daughter, Bener-ib, or Sweetheart.

From the time when Menes died until a man named Zoser came to the throne, some six hundred years later, the Pharaohs who ruled the country had a constant struggle to keep the two kingdoms together. Now in Zoser's court there was a man called Imhotep, who was so wise and so loved that he was remembered for hundreds of years by the Egyptians. They put up a temple to him and even worshiped him as one of their gods. Perhaps Imhotep, who remained with Zoser throughout his entire reign, guided him in the ruling of his kingdom.

AN EARLY EGYPTIAN KING SMITES HIS ENEMY—A BEDOUIN FROM SINAI

At least we know that Zoser succeeded in firmly uniting the kingdoms of the North and South, which Menes had ruled, and in gaining the love and admiration of his subjects. Even two thousand years after his death he was still remembered.

It was during the eighteenth year of Zoser's reign that a terrible famine arose in Egypt. There came a year when the farmers watched in vain for the flooding of the Nile. When the waters at last came, they barely rose over those lands near the banks. Wells were empty, and many men had no fertile fields. Summer—that time of rejoicing—became a time of worry and of sorrow. Food was scarce that winter and scarcer still the next, as the Nile lay quiet, a sullen muddy stream. No rain fell.

There is a story carved on the rocks of the first cataract of the Nile, which contains this letter from Zoser to one of his princes:

"This is to inform you of the sorrow which has afflicted me upon my great throne, and how my heart aches because of the great calamity that has occurred, for the Nile has not risen properly for seven years. There is a scarcity of corn, there are no vegetables, there is no food of any kind, and every man is stealing from his neighbors. When men desire to walk, they have not the strength to move, the child wails, the young man drags his legs, the hearts of the old are crushed with despair, their legs fail them so that they fall to the ground, their hands clutching their stomachs. My counsellors have no advice to give, and when the granaries are open nothing but air issues from them. Everything is in a state of ruin."

The letter goes on to tell how Zoser asked the prince if he knew where the Nile rose and to what god he must go for help. The prince, the story tells us, answered the letter in person, going at once to the king. He explained to Zoser that the water of the river was controlled by the great god, Khnum, and he advised the king to call on the god in his temple, which was on an island called Elephantine. Zoser took the prince's advice and went at once to the temple. Entering, he bowed low and made his offerings to the gods. Then he knelt before the statue of Khnum, told him how the people of his country were suffering, and asked his help. When the king had finished speaking, the statue of the god leaned forward and replied. It told Zoser that the god was angry because his temple had been neglected and was in such bad repair. The king promised hastily that the temple should be rebuilt at once and Khnum promised in return good harvests in the future.

If you should ever go to Egypt and see the rock on which this story is carved, try to realize that at a time when men in Europe were hardly more than savages, there was a great king in Egypt who so loved his people that he was willing to go to any lengths, even to asking help of a prince, to relieve their distress.

Under the wise rule of Zoser, Egypt was a country firmly united. All the troubles at home were settled for the time being, so that when Snefru came to the throne, many years after Zoser's death, he could turn his attention to other things than government. Up the Nile, just south of Egypt, lived tribes of wild black men. For many years they had overrun the south of Egypt and raided small Egyptian towns. No one had yet been able to subdue them. Snefru ordered that several large boats, each nearly one hundred and seventy feet in length, be built; also sixty smaller ones. When the boats were completed, he sent out a strong expedition against the blacks; and he more than evened up the score against them, for his soldiers brought back seven thousand prisoners, to spend their lives in slavery. They also brought back twenty thousand cattle, sheep and goats. For a long time the blacks troubled Egypt no more.

When Snefru's victorious fleet returned from the south, he decided to send it on another mission. Traders from the north had brought with them tales of a land far off across the sea, where trees grew tall and strong, trees from which great planks could be cut. Now trees in Egypt were very scarce and what few there were, were knotty and scrubby. If Snefru wanted great ships he must have big trees. So forty vessels of his fleet set sail down the Nile and ventured out into the great unknown sea to the north, carrying the flag of Egypt for the first time to foreign shores. When the ships returned they were laden with great cedar logs from the forests of Lebanon. This, so far as we know, was the first trading that had ever been done by sea.

More ships were sent to far off Sinai, to bring copper ore back from the mines. And just as the Pharaoh had punished the blacks who had attacked his people in the south; so he punished the wandering Bedouin tribes, who for hundreds of years had robbed and plundered the Egyptian miners. Under Snefru's rule, Egypt became the richest and the most powerful country in the world. His reign was the beginning of years of peace and plenty.

FARMERS CUTTING DOWN THEIR GRAIN

IV

THE MASTER BUILDERS

(Time, About 2900–2625 B.C.)

Khufu, son of Snefru, was strong and proud. Like all the others before and after him, one of his first thoughts was the building of his tomb. He wanted one larger than any that had yet been built, so large that it could be seen for miles around, so large that in the years to come all who looked at it would wonder at the greatness of the man who built it.

So he set to work. He and his builders laid their plans. Now the style in tombs had changed, and the fashion of the day was to build in the shape of a pyramid. Khufu planned that each side of his pyramid was to be seven hundred and fifty-five feet long—in our measurement—and that it was to rise until it was four hundred and eighty-one feet high. This pyramid was to be of solid stone, one block laid on top of the other, all of it done by hand. Each block would weigh about two and a half tons. And when the work was completed, more than two million of those blocks had been used!

It was a tremendous task. The huge stone blocks had first to be taken from the quarries on the other side of the Nile.

Throughout the land, Khufu sent out his call for men. But being a wise king, as well as an ambitious one, he called them at a time when the waters of the Nile were at their highest, and there was no farming to do. They came—a hundred thousand of them at a time—put up their mud huts on the edge of the desert and set to work.

Day after day the air rang with the sound of workmen's voices, calling to one another as they pried and hewed and hammered loose the great rocks. Stone masons chipped and levelled and polished the sides until the blocks were ready for use. Next they must be loaded on sledges and pulled through the sand to the river bank, where they were transferred to boats or rafts. Then began the perilous trip across the Nile. Men pulled on their oars and hoped that the wind would continue strong to help them with their heavy loads.

Meanwhile, hundreds of other workmen had been constructing a huge ramp or causeway on the opposite shore, which led from the river up to the site of the pyramid. Each of the massive blocks, after it had been taken from the raft, was hauled along the ramp and shoved into its place.

Year after year the work went on, but only during that season when the waters of the Nile were high and farming was impossible. There was a constant procession of boats and rafts bringing the huge stones across the Nile. Then they were dragged up the causeway to the base of the pyramid and hauled into position.

We do not know by what means these heavy

blocks were placed one on top of another. Probably stone ramps were constructed which zigzagged up the sides of the pyramid as it grew in height. Heavy ropes were fastened to each block and the hot sun shone down on the hundreds of men, as they pulled on the ropes in unison, keeping time to the cries of the overseers or to the beating of little hand drums. And always ahead of them ran others who poured oil or water in the path of the stones so that they might slide more easily.

At night the workmen flung down their tools, braced the blocks so that they could not slide back, and went to their mud huts for a well-earned rest. They must have wondered, as they sat under the stars, over their supper of bread and onions and beer, how things were going with their wives and children at home. And surely they often discussed the strange new tomb that their Pharaoh was building, and wondered how many more summers' work would be needed to finish it.

One of the caissons used in building these pyramids was unearthed not long ago by Mr.

Ambrose Lansing, of the Metropolitan Museum of Art of New York. It is made of stone and brick and through its use men were able to sink shafts down through the loose sand. Just such a caisson is used in this country in constructions like the Holland Tunnel which runs under the Hudson River.

Khufu's men worked well. The huge blocks which form the walls were fitted so closely together that even today not the blade of a knife can be inserted where they join. After all the stones had been laid in their places, the whole building was finished with a casing of smooth polished blocks of limestone. There it stood, white and shining in the sun. And nowhere on all four sides could any man tell that up toward the top on the northern side was a trap-door made of stone, which opened into a passage-way, leading to the chamber where the body of Khufu was to lie.

It was while the building of the pyramid was going on that Khufu received news from his vizier (a sort of Prime Minister) that made him rage.

Snefru and Hetep-heres, the father and mother of Khufu, slept side by side, he in his pyramid, she in her tomb—in the old cemetery at Dashur. They were forgotten for the moment by the people, the court and perhaps even by Khufu himself, whose interest lay now in the building of his own pyramid.

Few people now lived at Dashur. There were only the police guards, the priests who took care of the old tombs, and the workmen who were busy preparing new tombs. Everything was peaceful. There was plenty of time for those few guardians of the cemetery to think and to talk among themselves of the people buried there and the treasure lying with them. You can guess what happened. A few of the bolder and more wicked men banded themselves together and, one dark night, they crept softly to the tomb of Hetep-heres, the mother of the Pharaoh. Some among them must have known how the tomb was constructed, for they broke and bored their way through, until they had reached the burial chamber. There, by the light of their flickering torches, which threw weird shadows on the walls, they saw the alabaster sarcophagus that held the body of the queen. Near by stood her bed, her carrying chair, cased in gold, her armchairs, pottery and jars of alabaster, and her gold-covered chests.

Not an instant did the thieves hesitate. Knowing that the most valuable objects, the jewels, were buried with the body, they made straight for the sarcophagus. With their metal chisels they chipped and pried until they could lift the lid. Then they snatched the jewels which lay placed neatly in position on the mummy and removed the mummy itself.

It may have been the next day or it may have been several days later, that someone reported the robbery to the vizier. Hastily calling together some of his trusted friends, he hurried to the tomb and saw the rifled sarcophagus. He knew that if Khufu ever heard of what had happened, he and all of his friends would probably lose their lives in a most unpleasant manner. Cleverly they laid their plans to keep it from his knowledge. The lid of the sarcophagus was replaced and one of their men was left to guard the tomb.

Undoubtedly the vizier told Khufu that some evil persons had attempted to rob the chamber of His Majesty's mother; that fortunately His Majesty's faithful servants had been on guard, and that the robbers had been caught and killed at once. He very likely suggested to Khufu that it might be well if the body of his mother were placed in a new tomb at Gizeh, beside His Majesty's own new and beautiful pyramid.

We can well believe that Khufu wasted no time and as soon as possible men were sent to transfer the things in the chamber—the bed, the chairs, the chests, the beautiful vases and the sarcophagus. Carefully they were deposited in their new resting place near the pyramid. New offerings were made of food and sacred beer to the soul of Queen Hetep-heres and the tomb was sealed and covered. So Khufu was tricked, and the vizier and his friends were saved.

On March 3, 1927, after almost two years

devoted to the painstaking removal of other objects from the tomb, Dr. Reisner and his assistants from the Museum of Fine Arts in Boston, opened the sarcophagus of Queen Hetep-heres and found it empty. By a fine piece of detective work they were able to figure out for the first time what trick had probably been played on Khufu thousands of years ago.

Surely Khufu himself never knew of the robbers who destroyed his mother's tomb, nor guessed that later he too would share the same fate. Time, the enemy of the work of all men, wore down his pyramid. The casing stones fell out or were removed. The secret entrance was discovered—and for hundreds of years the burial chamber of the great Pharaoh, who took such pains that it should never be so, has lain empty.

When Khufu's son, Khafra, came to the throne he, too, built himself a pyramid. It was not as large as his father's though he had it placed on higher ground so that it looked larger. The base he cased with red granite, which he brought from far up the Nile.

If you should ever see Khafra's pyramid, you will find standing near it a monument, which for hundreds of years has caused the world to wonder. No one has yet been able to determine when or how the monument was made, yet it bears Khafra's name and perhaps was built during his reign.

A mass of rock has been hewn and carved until it resembles the form of a great lion, lying with his paws outspread. The head of the lion is carved like the head of a Pharaoh, and the face, which was once painted bright red, looks like the face of Khafra. Between the paws of the lion, stand a temple and an altar to the sun-god. The old Egyptians called this monument Hu, which meant "hewn thing." The Greeks, hundreds of years later, called it the Sphinx, and so it is known to us.

There it has stood for thousands of years, watching over the desert, a great figure, seventy feet high and nearly one hundred and fifty feet long. Drifting sands have almost covered it at times, and once, only a few hundreds of years ago, a Mohammedan, feeling that the Sphinx

THE SPHINX WITH A PYRAMID IN THE BACKGROUND

stood for something of which his religion did not approve, attempted to destroy the face, which was already battered by time.

There is an old Egyptian folk tale which tells the story of how Khufu, in an idle hour, sent for a magician to come to entertain him. After the magician had amused Khufu with some of his tricks, the Pharaoh began to question him about the future, just as we today ask the fortune-tellers what is coming to us. But the news for Khufu was not pleasing.

The magician told him reluctantly that somewhere in his kingdom three children would be born, who would become kings of Egypt. This made Khufu unhappy, for he hoped as all kings do that his children and his grand-children and his great-grand-children would keep the kingdom in their power. Seeing his distress, the magician went on to tell him, "Thy son shall reign, then thy grandson —after that one of these three children."

We do not know how much of the magician's prophecy came true, but it seems that Menkaure, who built the third and last pyramid, was the last of Khufu's family to rule Egypt. The kings who followed him were chosen by the priests of the country, who gradually had become very powerful.

From that time on, the power of a Pharaoh was seldom as great as it had been. As the country grew and the duties of the Pharaohs became more pressing, more and more responsibility was taken over by the nobles and priests. Some of them were loyal to their king and proud to serve him, while others became trouble-makers, grasping power for themselves whenever possible, and occasionally even reaching the throne and ruling the entire country.

One of those nobles who served his country under several Pharaohs, and who has left us a record of his life, was named Uni.

V

A WALK WITH UNI

(Time, About 2625 B.C.)

When Uni was a little boy, he lived in the palace and grew up with the children of King Teti, and it must have been rather a nice time and place in which to grow up. Like all other children in Egypt, Uni ran about with no clothes on whatever, except perhaps a narrow girdle or a thread tied about his waist. With a warm sun always shining, why should one need clothes? All day long he played about the courtyard with his toys, or did his lessons with the other boys. Reading and writing he had to learn, and some arithmetic. He must know how to throw a spear or boomerang, and how to hold his bow so that the arrow would go straight to the mark. Learning to swim was very important, too, for a boy who might go out on the Nile in a light boat made of papyrus reeds, to spear fish or to catch a hoopoe bird. When lessons were over, there was always the pool in the garden filled with gaily colored fish to splash in, or he might play with the other children of the palace. Perhaps the pet grasshoppers, kept so carefully in their cages of painted rushes, could be made to race. And if the grasshoppers sulked, he could play at hand-ball or leap-frog with the other boys. Sometimes he could watch the women of the palace dance to the music of the harp or flute. Their dances were slow and graceful.

Dinner time meant as much to Uni as it does to us, and he probably had just as many good things to eat. We find a record of one man who wanted "ten different kinds of meat, five kinds of poultry, sixteen kinds of bread and cakes, six kinds of wine, four kinds of beer, eleven kinds of fruit, besides all sorts of sweets and many other things" left for him in his tomb after his death. So we can be sure that Uni stuffed himself on feast days, just as boys and girls of today do on Thanksgiving.

The food was served in dishes of alabaster, copper, gold or silver, and was eaten with beautifully-carved spoons or with the fingers. And if Uni or any other little boy ate too many of the sweets or cakes, his mother gave him castor oil. She didn't mix it with orange juice, and let him swallow it quickly. She gave him castor oil berries, and made him chew them slowly and swallow them down with beer.

It was a busy world that Uni lived in, and sometimes he went out among the people to watch what they were about. There were so many interesting things to see! Let us go with him.

Here is the large estate of one of the nobles of the palace. The sky is very blue and the sun is very bright. Slaves are harvesting great fields of wheat or barley. When that grain was planted, the farmers used a wooden plow which was drawn by two oxen. One man ran beside the oxen, prodding the great beasts with a short stick when they were stubborn, while the plowman guided the share in the furrow.

Now the grain is being harvested. Men swing their short sickles in rhythm, keeping time to the shrill music of a pipe. Because the day is unusually warm, they are permitted to stop sometimes to drink deeply from the mugs of beer, which one of the servants passes among them. But the eye of the overseer is on them, and once the beer is gone they are quickly at work again, some binding the corn in sheaves, others loading it on little donkeys that will carry it to the threshers.

One hears constantly the creak of the shadufs, as the slaves lift the water from pool to pool and pour it on the gardens, where peas, lentils, radishes, lettuces, beans and other vegetables are flourishing.

Large herds of cattle are grazing contentedly in the pastures, and the stupid sheep nibble at the coarse grass. Later when the flood comes and the waters of the Nile rise, all these cattle will be driven hastily to higher ground, and it will be a lucky farmer who does not lose some of his cows or sheep in the excitement.

Some of the women slaves sit in the door-

FISHERMEN PULLING IN A FULL NET FROM THE NILE

ways of their thatched huts, spinning and weaving cotton, muslin or linen. The linen they weave is so fine that it looks almost like silk, and it is so strong that, thousands of years later, men will look at it and marvel that it is still whole.

On another excursion Uni stops to watch

the river. It is a lively place. Boats and barges of all sizes continually pass up and down. There are boats laden with grain or with cattle, barges which ride low in the water under their

burden of stone from the quarries. From the pleasure boats with their gay sails comes the sound of singing oarsmen, or the tinkling music of the harp. The kitchen boats drift along behind, and the breeze carries the odor of the delicious meal which is being prepared for the master. The little skiffs, made of long bundles of papyrus reeds, skim lightly through the water, which sparkles in the sun. It is a busy river and a gay one.

When Uni goes on one of these boats to the town, and walks about the narrow streets, he finds so many things going on that he can hardly watch them all. Cabinet-makers are busy making beautiful inlaid and carved furniture, which will be used by the nobles and the king, or more simple furniture for the common people. Smiths are forging tools of copper, making nails, bolts and hinges, or beating out wonderful weapons. Fine metal workers fashion heavy necklaces, shape rings for the ear or finger, and inlay with enamel or precious stones the large breast jewels. Engravers are busy at the heavy gold and silver cups and plates, which will later be used at some high feast. Potters are turning their wheels, or painting vases and bowls which have already been baked, in lovely greens, yellows, blues and reds. Glass blowers sit at their work making vases, cups, bottles and beads. Tanners treat the hides which have been brought in to them, or dye them beautiful colors so that they may be used to cover chairs and stools. In another shop Uni sees men making out of colored paste clever imitation pearls, amethysts and emeralds which will gladden the heart of some young Egyptian girl, who cannot afford the real jewels worn by the noble ladies.

The toy-maker's shop is a busy place. Children gaze longingly at the wooden dolls, some of them with real hair, staring stiffly from the shelves. Here are crocodiles that will move their jaws up and down with slow, crunching movements; wooden toys on wheels, which can be pulled along the paved path of the garden; balls of all kinds; and hundreds of brilliant pottery animals.

The noise in the market streets is terrific. The people crowd about, exchanging one thing for another. One will give a bundle of onions for a fan, a wooden box for a string of beads, or a piece of pottery for a jar of ointment. Sometimes gold and copper rings of a definite weight are used as money. Clerks and secretaries are busy keeping accounts, writing out orders and receipts, and drawing up contracts.

As Uni wanders from the crowded market-place down to the river, he hears from the ship-yards the steady pound-pound of the shipwright's hammer, as great vessels and heavy cargo boats are made ready for the Nile. Although Egypt is poor in wood, as her only trees are not good timber trees, enough is brought from other countries to fill the needs of the people. It is interesting to watch the builders bore holes along the edges of the boards and lace them together with heavy rope, covering the seams with thick layers of tar or pitch.

Here, rushing down the road, running, tumbling, falling over each other, calling, whistling, Uni sees the boys who have just been let out of school. All the morning they have sat cross-legged on the floor, learning to read and write. It is very hard to master hieratic, and the little boys spend many weary hours practising on limestone chips or pieces of broken pottery. With their reed pens they have copied carefully in their papyrus rolls model letters, proverbs and compositions, little dreaming that, hundreds of years later, men will dig up their copy-books and smile sympathetically over their mistakes.

School masters are strict in Old Egypt. "Be not slack and spend not a day in idleness, or woe betide thy limbs! Enter into the methods of thy teacher and hear his instructions." "The ear of a boy is on his back and he hearkeneth when he is beaten." This is only a little advice to which these boys have had to listen. But the morning is over, school is out and our walk with Uni is finished.

A CONTEST OF STRENGTH BETWEEN TWO BULLS

VI

A LOYAL SERVANT

(Time, About 2565 B.C.)

Children of Egypt grew up much more quickly than do children of today. Uni was only about ten years old when he "assumed the girdle," which meant that his days of play were over and that he must soon become a man. He was then given an unimportant office in the court. It probably looked very important to him at the time, but when he was grown up he wrote of it, "I became an inferior custodian in the domains of the Pharaoh." This was while King Teti was still alive. After King Teti's death, Uni still remained one of the trusted servants under the next Pharaoh and even under the next, becoming a famous leader and commander.

It was during the reign of King Pepi, that the sand-dwellers, those wild Arabs who to this day prefer to make their living by armed robbery, gave more trouble than usual. Their raids on the people living in the Delta grew bolder, and they even attacked the mining expeditions in Sinai, so that many complaints came to the Pharaoh. Pepi, looking among his officers for a man who was strong and able, chose Uni. He told him to collect an army and to march against the sand-dwellers. Uni gathered his army "of tens of thousands" mostly from among the Negroes in Nubia, for the Egyptians were not fond of fighting. With his black army he marched upon the Arabs. It was a wonderful army, for he wrote of them in records which he left, "Not one of the army quarreled with his neighbor, not one of them plundered dough or sandals from the wayfarer; not one of them took bread from the city, not one thereof took any goat from any people."

After the Arabs had been defeated and sent back to their desert, Uni led his army back to Egypt in triumph. Of the return he wrote:

"This army returned in safety after it had hacked up the land of the Sand-Dwellers.

"This army returned in safety after it had overturned its strongholds.

"This army returned in safety after it had cut down its fig-trees and its vines.

"This army returned in safety after it had slain troops there in many tens of thousands.

"This army returned in safety after it had carried therefrom a great multitude as living captives.

"His Majesty praised me on account of it above everything."

But the Arabs only waited until his back was turned before they again began to raid and rob. Five times Uni led his army against them before they were subdued.

Uni led a long life and a useful one. When King Pepi died, his little son, Mernere, was only seven years old. He needed strong men and wise to help him govern his country. Of course, he chose Uni, who had been so faithful under his father. Not only did he appoint

A KING BREAKS GROUND FOR A NEW CANAL

him "Master of the Royal Footstool and Bearer of the Royal Sandals," but he gave him another and much more important title, "Duke and Governor of the South Land."

Just below the First Cataract was the island of Elephantine, where the Nile went rushing through the rapids around huge piles of black granite. The valley of the cataract was called the "Door of the South," and beyond it only the bravest dared to go, for there lived the wild tribes of Nubia, the Wawat and the Kush. They were dark-skinned, kinky-haired men, fierce and savage, who lived in rude mud huts along the river. The Egyptians did not want their land, for little of it was fertile, but the hills and valleys on the west were rich in gold and iron. Also through their country ran the trade routes to the Sudan. Much gold and ivory, many ebony logs, ostrich feathers, panther skins and slaves were brought by caravan from the Sudan, so it was very important that the Egyptians have some control over these people.

On the island of Elephantine lived a family of brave and adventurous nobles, who guarded this entrance to Egypt. The head of the family was called the "Keeper of the Door of the South." It was the duty of these nobles to guard the entrance and to protect it from the blacks. Shortly after Mernere became Pharaoh, he sent Uni out to these granite quarries just above the cataract to get some materials for his tomb. So well had these nobles succeeded in keeping the fierce black men subdued, that Uni was able to go up the Nile and to obtain what he was after with only one warship to protect him.

Mernere was so encouraged by the success of this expedition that he sent Uni back again —this time on a much more difficult mission. He was ordered to dig five canals, which were to form a safe passage through the cataract, so that boats might pass on in safety up the Nile.

This was more of a task than it sounds. Of course, no one in his senses would tackle the Nile cataracts when the river was high, and even at half-height it would be perilous. Imagine the waters rushing and pouring over the rocks, dashing in treacherous whirlpools and unexpected currents. Here the men had to form human chains—one clinging to the land, the others standing, waist-deep in the swirling water, slipping and falling, but still keeping a firm grip on the end-man, who pounded and hammered or held the drill, churning sand and water under his copper tools.

Here Uni proved his leadership and his skill, too, for not only did he and his men dig all five canals, but they constructed three tow-boats and four barges as well, in one year. The blacks provided the acacia wood and perhaps even helped in the building of the boats. Large hollows were dug in the quarry beds of the Nile, when the waters were low. Then the barges were built in these hollows and great slabs of granite were loaded on them. As the season changed and the waters of the Nile began to rise, the barges rose with them and at last floated free. Using the canals which he had just completed, Uni went home in triumph.

NEGRO PRISONERS FROM THE SUDAN

VII

HARKHUF, THE GREAT EXPLORER

(Time, About 2565–2475 B.C.)

"The king praised me, my father made a will in my favor, I was a man of worth, beloved of his father, blessed by his mother, one whom all his brothers loved. I gave bread to the hungry, clothing to the naked, and I ferried him who possessed no boat."

So begins the record of the life of another great Egyptian. Over four thousand years ago it was carved on the front of a rock-cut tomb, in the cliffs of Aswan, near the island of Elephantine. The tomb belonged to Harkhuf, one of the first real explorers of the world.

Like many men of today he held many offices and before he died he had become, among other things a duke, a priest, a judge, a leader of caravans and a governor of the South.

Harkhuf was one of that family of nobles at Elephantine, who had so well guarded the "Southern Door" of Egypt from the savage tribes of Wawat and Kush. While he was still a very young man—too young to make such an expedition alone—Mernere sent him with his father to the land of Yam, which was far down in the south near the Second Cataract, to build a high-road through the desert, for the trading caravans. Uni and the lords of Elephantine had succeeded in gaining some control over the blacks near the First Cataract. But no one had yet dared go farther south by way of the river though of course it would have been an easier and more pleasant way than the long trip across the desert, for those who were bringing things from the Sudan. Therefore, good desert highways were necessary.

For seven long months Harkhuf's road-builders toiled under the hot sun, constructing the highway that would make easier the journey of those traders. In the cool of the night they sat around their camp-fires under the stars and talked of the caravans that would pass over their road, bearing ivory and feathers and precious metals to Egypt. They spoke with envy of the rich and powerful nobles who would some day use these things. They argued as men do today about their government and their taxes. They wondered if their sons were doing well in school and if their daughters were helpful and obedient at home. And at last, the road finished, they turned their faces toward home.

But there was to be no rest for Harkhuf, for Mernere sent him forth again almost at once, this time in charge of his own expedition.

It took great courage in those days to journey into the desert. The Egyptians knew so little of what the land beyond their own country was like, that they called it the "Land of Ghosts." Not only did they fear the wild tribes of black men who lived along the river bank, but they believed also that they might be attacked at any time by strange and dreadful animals, which they imagined lurked in the shadows, ready to spring on them.

Harkhuf pushed on bravely through the desert, leading his men over miles of burning sands, until he reached at last the land of the Mazoi. This was the end of the world to the Egyptians. They knew nothing of what was beyond. Still Harkhuf forged ahead into the unknown world. His men must often have wanted to turn back, as did those men who sailed with Columbus so many hundreds of years later. But he kept on until he had made a great circuit of all the western countries, exploring and investigating those strange lands.

He came back at last to Yam, where he collected the gifts that he had ordered previously for his Pharaoh. It was a long and disagreeable journey from Yam back to his own country and meant many days of marching through the hot desert, so Harkhuf decided to continue his explorations and go home by way of the river. This the Egyptians had never done before, for they still feared the kinky-haired black men, who robbed and plundered where they could. But Harkhuf led his men so boldly and bravely through the little mud-thatched villages, that the black men watched amazed and never dared to attack the caravan.

The third time Harkhuf was sent to Yam he took the Oasis Road which led to the little oasis at Kurkur. When he reached Kurkur, no chieftain came forth to welcome him. The people of the village told him that their chief had gone off to settle a quarrrel with the Tehennu, a white skinned race, related to the Libyans. He had gone, they declared, to knock those Tehennu out of the world—"as far as the western corner-post of the canopy of Heaven." Harkhuf thinking, no doubt, that if any one conquered the Tehennu it should be himself, hurried on after the angry chieftain. When he had overtaken him, he persuaded him to make peace with the Tehennu and return to his own country. They went back together to Kurkur.

So impressed was the savage chieftain with Harkhuf's bravery and wisdom, that he offered to send a band of his finest warriors to act as the Egyptian's escort, on his return to his own country.

With this splendid guard which would protect him from the raids and robberies of the unfriendly savages along the way, Harkhuf took back to Egypt more treasure than ever before. On three hundred asses (there were no camels or horses in Egypt at that time) he loaded fragrant incense, ebony bars, grain, panther skins, ivory boomerangs, and many other valuable things.

When he and his richly-laden train, with his own soldiers and the tall, black warriors from Yam, reached the river towns, no attempt was made to rob them, though surely the eyes of the natives must have popped at the sight of such wealth. In fact, the chieftain of Arthet, as he watched them march into his territory, realized that Harkhuf was by far the most important noble or caravan leader who had ever passed through his country, and he brought gifts of bulls and small cattle, and even went with him part way toward home. When Harkhuf reached the First Cataract, he found

THESE DONKEYS ARE BEING DRIVEN TO THE MARKET PLACE WHERE THEIR OWNERS WILL BARTER OR EXCHANGE THEIR GOODS FOR OTHER THINGS

that, just as we today send out a welcome to greet our brave explorers, so Mernere had sent a ship to meet him, bearing date wine, cakes, bread and beer. He went in state to the capital.

Such an impression had been made upon the black men by the expeditions of Uni and Harkhuf, it was decided that Mernere, the boy king, who was now about eleven years old, should go to Aswan to show himself in all his glory to the river chieftains. So in the cool of the year, when the journey could be made most

comfortably, he made the trip up the Nile. There on the east bank of the river, within sound of the First Cataract, he met the black chieftains, who, awed by the splendor of the young king, bowed before him and praised him. No king had ever before ventured so far south and there on the rocks two inscriptions were cut, which told of his coming.

Whether this trip up the Nile was too much

for the little Pharaoh we do not know, but we do know that shortly after this he died, and Pepi the Second, his little half-brother, only six years old, was placed on the throne.

The nobles must have been very loyal, and Pepi's mother, who surely acted for him in ruling the country, must have been very wise, for there was no disturbance in the land and no one attempted to rob the little prince of his throne.

During the second year of Pepi's reign, Harkhuf, the great explorer, returned from his fourth trip to the Sudan. He brought a gift to the little Pharaoh—a tiny dwarf—a funny little bandy-legged creature, who had been trained to dance. As soon as he reached Elephantine, Harkhuf wrote to Pepi, telling him of his gift. The little boy's joy knew no bounds. Excited and delighted at the thought of really owning such a curious, little creature, he wrote, probably with the help of his mother and a scribe, a long letter of which this is part:

"I have noted the contents of your letter which you sent to me, the king at the palace, in order that

I may know that you have returned from Yam, with the troops which were with you. . . . You said in your letter that you have brought back from the Land of the Ghosts, a pigmy of the kind employed there in the dances of their gods. . . . Come northward to the court at once, and bring with you this pigmy of the sacred dances, which you have brought alive and in good condition and health from the Land of the Ghosts, to please and delight the heart of the King of Upper and Lower Egypt, who lives forever. When he goes with you on board the ship, appoint trustworthy people who shall remain near him on each side of the vessel; take care that he does not fall into the water. When he sleeps at night appoint trustworthy people who shall sleep beside him in his cabin; and make inspection ten times a night. My Majesty wants to see this pigmy more than all the gifts from the mines of Sinai or from the Land of Punt. . . . Orders have been sent to the governor of the New Towns, directing that the necessary supplies are to be taken from him by you at every store-city and every temple without stinting."

We are sure that the pigmy reached Pepi in safety and Harkhuf was richly rewarded. The faithful servant of the Pharaoh was so proud of this letter from his little king, that he had it engraved on the walls of his tomb. Some day perhaps you will see it there.

Harkhuf was only one of the many brave explorers who carried the name of Pepi II to far-off foreign lands. The lords of Elephantine continued their explorations south of Egypt among the black men. They went also to the Land of Punt, which was far to the south on the shores of the Red Sea. This was a doubly dangerous journey, for the men had to cross the desert, carrying with them enough lumber to build the boats which were to carry them down the coast. After they had made camp on the lonely shores of the sea, they built their ships. Often they were forced to fight off those desert thieves who lost no chance to rob all travelers.

In the north the royal fleets brought cedars from Lebanon and even landed on the island of Crete, which was a two or three days' sail from the northern coast of Egypt. When the Egyptian traders landed in Crete they found to their amazement a people almost as civilized as their own countrymen. They walked about on the paved streets, watching the people in the market place, wondering at the full, ruffled skirts of the women and the queer top-knots on the heads of the men. They marveled at the bull fights, and gasped in astonishment when they saw the boy and girl toreadors leaping lightly over the enraged animals. And when they returned to their own country they took with them many stories of these wonders. They took, also, a knowledge of a new metal, for the men of Crete had discovered that by mixing tin with their copper they could forge bronze weapons far stronger and more powerful than any they had made before.

And so Egypt might have gone on, exploring strange lands and conquering her neighbors either by trade or war, becoming more powerful than any other country, had it not been for trouble at home.

Pepi reigned a long time—too long. Historians tell us that his reign lasted ninety years or more. During his last years he was an old and feeble man, who had outlived all his faithful nobles. He was surrounded by young lords, eager to get the power of the throne into their own hands, anxious not for the good of Egypt, but for the good of themselves. So with his death ended one of the greatest periods in Egyptian history.

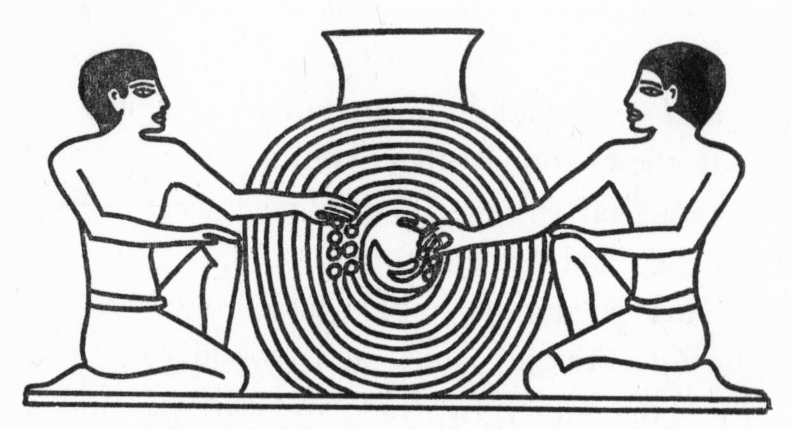

AN OLD EGYPTIAN GAME CALLED "THE VASE"
It was played on a circular board with marbles

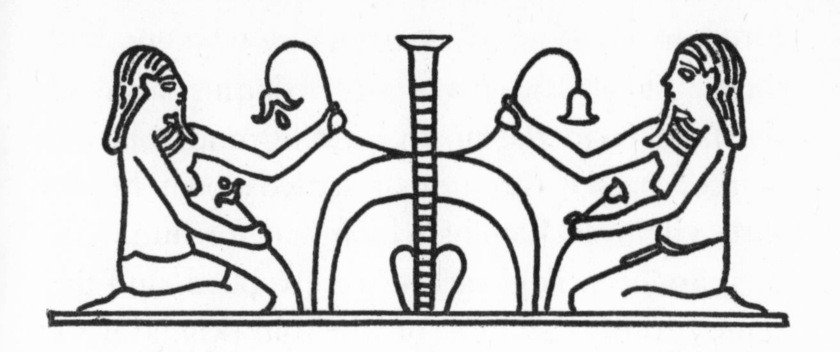

VIII

DARK DAYS

(Time, About 2475–1935 B.C.)

And now dark days fell upon the country, for the ambitious nobles grew more and more powerful. Each man carried out his own desires. He was busy snatching more land, ruling more slaves, and fighting with his neighbors. There was no time to explore, to carry on trade with foreign lands, or to defend the country from its enemies. The kinky-headed blacks from the south pushed down the Nile, past the canals at the First Cataract, which Uni had built and which were now crumbling to pieces. They destroyed the little farms, captured the farmers, and killed those who opposed them. The wild tribes of Bedouins invaded the land from the north, raiding and robbing as they passed through or settled down in the little villages. Tombs which had for hundreds of years been held sacred were robbed, and the huge granite statues of the old kings were deliberately smashed to bits. For many years there was no one in the land strong enough to guide the country, and while the nobles flourished everywhere, there was distress among the people. Hunger, robbery, fighting and disorder made their lives miserable.

There was a man called Ipuwer who went to the king who was in power at the time, to tell him of the troubles of the people and to try to make the king realize the conditions in the country. Here is part of his complaint:

"The face is pale, for the bowman is ready and the wrong-doer is everywhere. The peasant goes out to plow with his shield in his hand. The servants say, 'Let us go out and steal.' The very bird-catchers are drawn up in the line of battle, and the fenmen carry their

AN EGYPTIAN SOLDIER CARRYING A LARGE SHIELD

shields. A man looks upon his son as his enemy and fights with his brother, or is killed at his brother's side. Men's hearts are violent. Plague rages throughout the land. Blood is everywhere, nor is Death lacking in victims. No craftsmen work, for the enemies of the land have spoiled its crafts. The country is a desert throughout; the provinces are laid waste; a foreign tribe from abroad has come into Egypt; and the Asiatics have become skilled in the fenmen's professions.

"The tribes from the desert have everywhere become Egyptians, and there are no real Egyptians left anywhere. The roads have to be guarded, for men lurk behind bushes until the benighted traveler comes along, so that they may plunder his baggage and take away what is upon him. He is belabored with blows of their sticks or wickedly slain. The robber is everywhere.

"Gates, columns and walls are consumed by fire, boxes of ebony are smashed to pieces, and precious acacia-wood is chopped up. Princes are hungry and in distress; noble ladies are hungry and their limbs are in a sad plight by reason of their rags; men eat grass and wash it down with water. Corn has perished on every side. No food is found even for the birds. Squalor is apparent throughout the land, and there is none whose clothes are white in these times. The Nile overflows, yet no one plows the land. Cattle are left to stray and there is none to gather them together. The laws of the courts of justice are cast out, men tread on them in public places. Offices are rifled and their census lists are carried off. Officials are murdered and their writings are taken away. All is in ruins. Men have dared to rebel against the Crown; a few lawless men have attempted to rid the land of its monarchy . . . There is no end of noise, yet laughter has ceased, and it is groaning that fills the land, mingled with lamentations."

It is not a pretty picture that Ipuwer paints of the affairs in his country. Yet as you grow older and read the histories of other countries, you will find that there is hardly a nation that has not gone through just such a period. It is a period when the people pray that some man may come, who is strong enough to lead them in their fight against hunger, panic and disorder, and to help them become organized again so that each man may have work and peace.

Such a man was Intef, a prince from the south, who took the first steps in reuniting Egypt. He succeeded after a difficult struggle in organizing and ruling the south of Egypt, with Thebes as his capital. Then Mentuhotep, his son, did as Menes had done so many hundreds of years before him—pushed on to the north and finally gained control of most of that country. From that time on, under four sturdy and energetic princes—all of them Mentuhoteps—Egypt became more and more firmly united, though she was still in the hands of many different rulers. But the years were long and difficult before there came a man strong enough to bring peace and order to the entire land.

Other countries were in trouble too. In far-off Palestine and the neighboring lands, famine stalked, spreading disease and terror, and people fell by the roadside from lack of food. Those who were strong enough gathered their things together and left their country, searching for a more friendly land. And so they came to northern Egypt, to the lands around the Delta, and settled there in great numbers. As a strong and husky boy might steal into the yard of a smaller boy and use his toys or steal his candy, so these Asiatics settled in the unprotected lands of the Egyptians, taking their farms and their crops. To make matters worse, the Nile was low and food was scarce. The Egyptians themselves were having a hard enough time to get along. The people in the Delta were unprotected, and the Pharaoh who was then ruling either would not, or could not, do anything about it. At last conditions became so unbearable that the people revolted and either deposed or killed their Pharaoh.

It was then that Amenemhet, who was at that time the vizier, came to the throne. Amenemhet was strong, energetic and wise. When he had settled the disturbances in the Delta and had driven out the Asiatics, he ordered the people to build a huge wall across the eastern caravan route and stationed guards there, who watched from the top of the wall all that was happening on either side. No more wanderers could enter Egypt, even to ask for water for their cattle.

After he had driven out the Asiatics and made it impossible for them to return, the new Pharaoh then decided to build himself a capital and a palace. He chose a place not far from Memphis, which he called Ithtowe, or "Captor of Two Lands." Here he built a fortified city and erected a palace with ceilings and walls like lapis lazuli and floors like silver. The building was ornamented with gold and guarded with doors of copper and bolts of bronze.

You may remember that Egypt was at this time a land made up of many, many small states or kingdoms, each ruled by a noble or a family of nobles surrounded by their own slaves. Amenemhet was wise enough to know that he could never gain the loyalty of these men, either for himself or for Egypt, by taking their lands or trying to suppress them. Therefore, he went among them, settling their quarrels, restoring land that had been unfairly taken, and winning them by gifts and promises of high position in his court. In this way he was able to band them together into a sort of league, which paid him tribute in time of peace and service in time of war. Gradually the affairs of the country began to straighten out and prosperity to return.

Once more the Nile teemed with life. Whole fleets of transports were needed to bear the tribute to the king. Gold was brought from Nubia, copper from the mines at Sinai, and granite from far up the Nile. Herds of cattle and loads of grain were carried to the stock-yards and granaries at the capital. Once more the caravans set out, and the Nubians knew again what it was to fear their northern neighbors.

Once more the Egyptian farmer planted his

grain, sure that he alone would reap it. The potter and the metal-worker, the carpenter and the tanner went about their work, sure that there would be a market for their goods. In the thatched mud huts of the peasants there was food enough for all. The air rang once again with the shouts of boys as they ran to school, or with the cries of happy children at play.

But there is always ingratitude in this world. And while Amenemhet, now an old man, was watching over Egypt, one of those nearest to him, a man whom he had helped and protected, was planning how to kill off the old king and to snatch the kingdom for himself.

It was after supper when the night had come, and the weary king lay on his couch for a short rest. He was almost asleep when he heard strange whisperings in the dark and the sound of men moving about. Alarmed, the brave old man sprang to his feet and, grasping the weapon of one of his attackers, he managed to hold them at bay, until others in the palace roused by the clash of arms and the noise of fighting brought him help.

Poor old Amenemhet! For many, many long years he had fought for and guided his people. Now he became so embittered at the attack on him by men whom he had thought to be his friends, that he was grim and gloomy for the rest of his life. He called no man his friend. Almost at once he sent for his oldest son, Sesostris, to come and rule beside him on the throne. He wrote him, describing the attack and his defense of himself and adding unhappily, "But there is no strength by night and one cannot fight alone, and success will not come without thee that protectest me."

Sesostris joined his father at once. He reigned with him for many years and the prosperity of the country increased. During the eleventh year of their reign together, it became necessary to send out an expedition into the western desert to punish the Libyans, who, like so many mosquitoes, were always buzzing about the frontiers of Egypt. Sesostris, leaving his father in the capital city, headed the expedition successfully, taking many prisoners and capturing huge herds of cattle.

One night as he and his soldiers camped in the desert on the homeward route, a runner stole breathlessly into camp, just as dark was falling. Straight to Sesostris he went, with the news that the old King Amenemhet had died. Now there were several men in Egypt who were only waiting for the old king's death, so that they might try to set themselves in his place. Some of them were Sesostris' own brothers, who were with him in the army. Sesostris, anxious to leave camp before any of them learned the news, quickly called to him those men whom he knew to be most loyal. Under cover of the darkness they hurried back to the palace, where he claimed the throne at once, establishing himself as ruler over all Egypt.

Now a younger brother of Sesostris, who was with him in the army, had laid his plans rather cleverly. He had arranged with a friend of his who remained at the palace, to be notified immediately and secretly of his father's death.

When he heard the news that night he also made haste to start for Ithowe. But Sesostris was ready for him and on his arrival he and his fellow conspirators were punished. There was no trouble in the palace or in the city.

A HUNTER SHOOTS FROM THE SHELTER OF A SCREEN
His attendant carries the quiver and a battle-axe

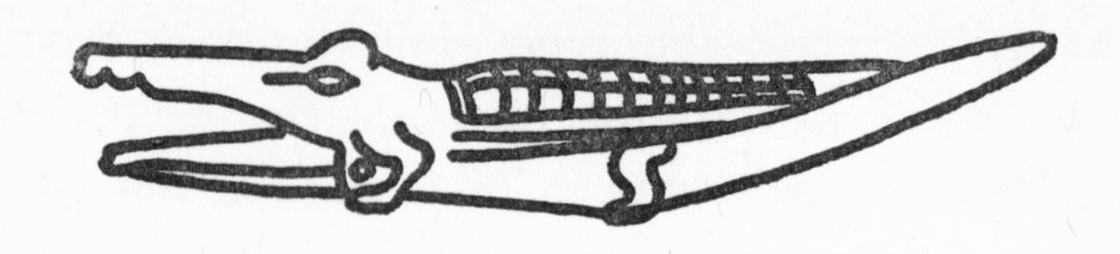

IX

THE ADVENTURES OF SINUHE

(Time, About 1980–1790 B.C.)

To one luckless soldier the unsuccessful plot, just related, brought many adventures.

Sinuhe was a friend of King Amenemhet and was also one of the most favored attendants of the Queen. And on that same fateful dark night he was in camp with the others. Now it happened that Sinuhe was standing near the tent of Sesostris and he overheard the carefully guarded news, which the runner had brought into camp. He had heard, also, of the conspiracy of the younger brother. At once the ever fearful question came to his mind—who would be king? If Sesostris were to rule, everything would be well, but if any one were to prove stronger than he, Sinuhe knew that his own life at Ithowe would not be worth living.

Many daggers would be aimed at his throat because of his friendship with the former court. At the thought of the turmoil and the fighting that would go on at the palace if Sesostris' place were disputed, the heart of Sinuhe almost stopped beating. Fear seized his throat and for a minute he seemed to lose his mind. Suddenly he knew that there was only one thing for him to do. He must escape from Egypt at once.

He did not stop for second thought, but rushed from the camp and, crouching low behind the bushes that grew at the side of the road, fled to the south, leaving the army far behind him. On and on he traveled through the dark night, until his weary legs would carry him no farther and he sank exhausted in an open field, where he slept till morning. At daybreak he was up again, with but one thought in his fear-ridden mind—to get far away from the fighting that he supposed was now going on at the capital. By late afternoon he had reached the Nile and there luck was with him, for tied to the shore he found a raft.

With the help of the west wind he ferried himself across the river.

When he reached the east bank of the Nile he left the raft and set off into the desert. On and on he plodded through the sand, working always to the north, until at last when his strength had almost given out, he came to the Prince's Wall, which Amenemhet had built in the first years of his reign, to keep out wandering Asiatics. Dropping to his knees, he crawled slowly and stealthily into the bushes near by, for the sentinels who always patrolled the top of the fortress were on guard, ready to challenge any wayfarers who might approach.

Here in the shadow of the bushes Sinuhe hid, grateful for the chance to rest, yet eager to reach the other side of the wall—to be really out of Egypt. And when night came with its kindly cover of darkness, he stole from his hiding place and crossed the wall. Once on the other side he staggered on. Ever on he urged his weary body, through the long night, leaving Egypt far behind, on and on, almost perishing from thirst. His throat was parched, his mouth dry, his tongue swollen, and his whole body cried out for water. At last he could go no farther and, as dawn was breaking, he sank exhausted on the sands. "So this is death," he thought.

But after he had lain there on the sands for some time he heard the lowing of cattle near by and the sound of men's voices. He opened his eyes and saw some Bedouins approaching. Luck, it seemed, was always with Sinuhe, for among the approaching men was a chieftain who had been in the Egyptian court a short time before, and he recognized the wanderer at once. The Bedouins brought the thirsty man some water, boiled some milk for him and took him to their tribe. Here he was treated with every kindness, but he would not remain with these people and after he had recovered from the trials of his journey he left them. Always eager to get far from Egypt, he went from one tribe to another, until finally he reached Keden, a village in Syria.

Not long after his arrival in Keden he received a message from Nenshi, the son of Amui, the prince of that country. This prince had heard of Sinuhe through some Egyptians who lived in his court, and he sent for him to come to him.

"Why have you come here?" asked Nenshi, the son of Amui, when Sinuhe was brought to him. "Has anything happened at the palace?"

"Amenemhet has gone down the Western Horizon and nobody knows what has happened at the palace as a result of this," answered Sinuhe. Then, perhaps feeling ashamed and wishing to give some reason for his cowardly flight from Egypt, he continued, "I was coming back from the campaign in the land of the Libyans when a certain piece of news became known to me, at which my brain reeled and my mind was no longer in my body, but led me away on the desert road. Yet nobody had spoken ill of me, nobody had spat in my face. I had heard no threatening word, nor had my name been cried by the mouth of the crier. I really do not know what brought me to this country."

Now it pleased the Prince very much that a

man of such education and one who had occupied such a high position in the court of the greatest country in the world should come into his land, and he invited Sinuhe to stay with him. Sinuhe accepted his invitation and in a short time he married the Prince's eldest daughter. Then the Prince, wishing to keep Sinuhe in his country, gave him his choice of homes. Sinuhe chose the land of Yaa—a delightful place where figs, grapes, olives, honey, fruits of all kinds, barley and wheat grew in abundance; where wine was more plentiful than water, and where great herds of cattle of all kinds were pastured. And soon Sinuhe was made chieftain of the tribe that occupied this country and gave up his Egyptian ways altogether. Like the Syrians whom he now ruled he lived in a tent, surrounded by the tents of his people, and he slept on the ground. Likewise he let his hair and beard grow long.

For many years he stayed in Syria and his sons grew up and became chieftains also, ruling the neighboring tribes. So well did Sinuhe attack and drive away the wandering tribes who continually molested the country that the Prince, who loved him well, finally made him commander of all the army.

But there was one man in Syria who was jealous of Sinuhe. He was a mighty man, a champion without equal, and all of Syria feared him. This man resented Sinuhe's rise to power. He decided that he would fight the Egyptian, rob him of all his cattle, shame him before his tribesmen, and drive him from the country. So he sent a challenge, which Sinuhe, after some misgivings, accepted.

That night Sinuhe strung his bow, tested his arrows, and sharpened his weapons. When morning came the Syrian arrived and half of the people of the country gathered to see the fight. All the people feared for the Egyptian, for no one had ever defeated the Syrian, who carried with him into the battle a shield, a battle-axe, and an armful of javelins.

Bravely Sinuhe advanced to meet his foe. With a cry the Syrian hurled his first javelins. But Sinuhe, quick on his feet as a cat, dodged them all in safety. Closer and closer they came to each other. When the Syrian was almost upon him, Sinuhe drew his bow and let loose an arrow. Right into the Syrian's neck it plunged and with a yell he fell forward on his nose, dropping his weapons. Hastily snatching the fallen battle-axe, Sinuhe leaped upon the back of the Syrian and killed him with a blow. Then amidst the excited cries of the onlookers he carried off the possessions of the fallen champion. He and his tribesmen rounded up the Syrian's cattle and took them for their own. From that time on, the Egyptian was more of a hero than ever and he became a very rich man.

But with all his honors and riches he was an unhappy man, for his mind turned always to the palace in Egypt and he longed to return to his own country.

"O, God," he prayed, "whatever god you are, who ordained this flight of mine, show mercy and bring me back to the palace. Perhaps you will grant me to see again the place where my heart dwells, for that thing is more important than that my body should be buried in the land where I was born. Oh, let the King of Egypt show mercy to me, that I may live by his mercy and greet once more the Lady of the Land, who is in the palace."

Now Sesostris, who still ruled in Egypt, heard of the desires of Sinuhe. Being a kindly man he sent at once a most gracious letter to the wanderer, bidding him come home at once, where he would be welcomed joyously. He wrote him, also, that even though he had deserted his own land, he would be buried as a real Egyptian should be, in a mummy case of gold. Oxen should draw his hearse, musicians should walk ahead, and dancers should perform the sacred dances of the tomb. The tomb itself, Sesostris wrote, would be erected among the tombs of the royal children. It was not fitting that any Egyptian should be buried among the Syrians, who only wrapped the body in a sheepskin and buried it under a mound of sand. There was one thing, however, that Sesostris insisted upon. Sinuhe must leave behind him, if he should decide to return to Egypt, all his wives and children.

Sinuhe was standing among his tribesmen when the letter came, and when it had been read aloud to him by the royal messengers, he flung himself on the ground, overcome with joy.

He made preparations at once for his return to Egypt. All his possessions, his cattle, his lands, his fruit trees and his wealth were divided among his sons. His eldest son took charge of his father's tribe.

Soon after the coming of the letter from the king, envoys arrived from Egypt to accompany the wanderer on his return. Many of the Syrians who wished to accompany their chief as far as possible on the journey, joined the party and they all set out across the desert. On their arrival at the Prince's Wall they found that the kindly Sesostris had sent his chief huntsman with boats filled with gifts for the Syrians who must now turn back. A great farewell feast was held in the shadow of the wall and then Sinuhe, bidding good-bye sorrowfully to his Syrian friends and relatives, crossed the wall alone and entered Egypt once more.

All night the return party sailed up the Nile. When they arrived at the capital next morning they found ten men at the landing place waiting to escort them to the palace. When the party reached the palace, Sinuhe saw the royal children gathered at the gateway to greet him. Straightway he was led to the courtyard and directed to the Audience Hall, where the Pharaoh, seated on his throne under an archway of gold, awaited him. At the sight of Sesostris, Sinuhe, overcome with fear and joy, flung himself at the feet of the king. His flesh trembled and his heart seemed to leave his body. He felt as he had on that fatal day so long ago when he had fled from Egypt. But one of the nobles raised the terror-stricken man to his feet and the King spoke to him kindly.

"So you have returned at last—you who have trodden the desert and wandered in the wilderness," he said.

But Sinuhe was afraid and could not speak. Then thinking to make his guest more comfortable, Sesostris sent for the Queen and the royal children. When the Queen, whom Si-

ONE OF THE PLEASURE BOATS WHICH SAILED THE NILE
Under the canopy sat the owner and his guests

nuhe had served so faithfully in his youth, saw him, she uttered a cry of joy. The children, who had heard many stories of the wanderer, looked at him in interest and began to plead with the King to be kind to him.

At last the King commanded that Sinuhe be taken to the house of one of the royal princes where he might refresh himself after his journey. Here, in a bathroom which was gaily decorated with beautiful scenes painted on the walls, he washed from his body the dust of the desert. There were many slaves about the house, all busy at their tasks, but they came at once to help Sinuhe with his dressing. First they shaved off his beard and combed his hair, then anointed him with precious ointment and clad him in fine linen. His old clothes, those which he had worn in Syria, were given to the sand-dwellers, and his bundles too were flung out into the desert. That night he slept on a bed for the first time in many years, and his heart overflowed with happiness. Waking next morning he was filled with joy at being again in his own country.

The generous King gave to him a house such as the nobles lived in. Meals were sent to his new home from the palace, and the royal children, who went often to hear from him strange tales of his years among far-off people, took him many gifts. Much more to his satisfaction, the work on his tomb and funeral statue was begun and Sinuhe, the wanderer, lived in honor and plenty for the rest of his days.

It may seem queer that an Egyptian who had fled from his own country, could go into a strange land and attain such fame and riches. But the Egyptian was a man of education and ability, and the Syrians among whom he settled were little more than savages. Just so, today, a young Englishman or American can sometimes go into wild parts of the world and establish himself as a person of importance.

While Sinuhe had been establishing himself in Syria, Sesostris, in Egypt, had been carrying on the good works of his father. And when he was an old man and well beloved, he too went down the Western Horizon, and his son

Amenemhet II became Pharaoh. For two hundred years this family ruled the country, and the common people as well as the nobles lived in comfort and prosperity.

Life was made easier for the miners and the traders. Even men of courage had dreaded the long, hot, difficult trip to the mines of Sinai. But they had dreaded more the constant attacks of the Bedouins—those pirates of the deserts. Great was the joy of the miners when they learned that they were to have barracks in which to live during the mining season, and that huge stone fortifications were to be erected for their protection. The trip to and from the mines was made less difficult when the Pharaoh ordered a canal dug between the Nile and the Red Sea. Then much of the journey could be made by boat. At the First Cataract, the canal which had been built by Uni and his men had long ago crumbled away. New canals were dug and once more the river way was opened to the traders.

The farmers, too, were helped. Fertile land, as you know, was found only along the banks of the river and there was not much of it. Not far from the Nile was a deep hollow in the desert called the Fayum. When the river was high, water flowed into this basin, forming a large lake. It occurred to some thoughtful man that the water could be pushed back, the lake made smaller, and the land so gained could be used for farming. A canal was dug which carried the water from the Nile to the lake, and then a huge dyke almost twenty miles long was built to keep it there. Nearly forty square miles of land was reclaimed in this way. Then, in the months when the Nile was the lowest, the water was released by means of gates and flowed back through the canal and down the river bed, carrying life to all the small farms through which it passed. This was the first storage reservoir of which history tells us.

It was a wonderful two hundred years for the people of Egypt. We know this by the things that tell of that time. Splendid temples were built to honor the gods. Jewelry as beautiful as any the world has ever known was made then. Magnificent statues of the Pharaohs, sometimes forty or fifty feet high, were carved in granite. Books of poetry, of travel, of stories and of fables were written.

Of course, men in other lands had by this time written books and carved statues and built temples too. In the valley of the Tigris and the Euphrates, to the northeast of Egypt, had been a land called Sumeria where there had been splendid cities—Lagash, Uruk and Ur. But war-like desert tribes had settled to the north of Sumeria in a land they called Akkad. They visited Sumeria and liking the cities there better than their own, they invaded and captured them. The land of Sumeria was no more.

Then from the city of Babylon, still farther north, came the great and wise king, Hammurabi. He took Akkad for his own and the land that had been Sumeria. He established himself as ruler over all the peoples of the lower valley, calling his kingdom Babylonia.

Ruled by King Hammurabi, Babylonia became a prosperous land. The king built roads and canals and schools. He established a postal system, and runners brought him letters written on baked clay tablets from all parts of his kingdom, regularly. He collected a library for his palace and gave his people a code of laws by which to live, sending clay copies of the laws throughout the land.

But Hammurabi died, as all kings do, and eight years after his death a tribe of mountain men called Kassites, descended upon the land. They raided and plundered and at last conquered the proud kingdom of Babylonia. For hundreds of years the land was a place of strife and chaos.

Far, far to the east of Egypt on the Indus river in a country which today we call India, men had lived in cities. One of them was the city of Mohenjo-daro. As yet, we know little about these cities and their history, for archeologists have been at work there for only a short time. But what they have found is proof that a real civilization existed there.

Still further to the east lies the land we call China. Here, according to the Chinese myths, men had for many years lived in cities, were beginning to develop their own art and to read and write. But those early Chinese kept no records and we do not know how far they were along the path of civilization, at the time when Amenemhet ruled the people of the Nile.

Egypt was, as far as we know now, the greatest country in the world—a nation of proud, intelligent, civilized people, even as measured by our ideas of today.

HEBREWS BRING ANIMALS AS GIFTS TO THE PHARAOH

X

THE SHIPWRECKED SAILOR

(Time, About 1790 B.C.)

Among the stories which were written in Egypt during this time of prosperity is the tale of "The Shipwrecked Sailor." The sailor himself tells the story to an Egyptian noble. He says:

"Now, my lord, I shall tell you what happened to me. I was going to the mines of the Pharaoh, and I went down on the sea on a ship of one hundred cubits long and forty cubits wide. There were on the ship one hundred and fifty sailors of the best of Egypt, men who knew the world and whose hearts were stronger than lions. They believed that our voyage would be a safe one. But as we approached the land the wind arose and threw waves eight cubits high. As for me, I seized a piece of wood, but those who were in the vessel perished. Not one remained. A wave threw me on an island.

"For three days I was there alone, without a companion beside my own heart. I laid me in a thicket and the shadow covered me. Then I looked about to try to find something to eat. I found there figs and grapes, all manner of good herbs, berries and grain, melons of all kinds, fishes and birds. Nothing was lacking. And I satisfied myself. When I had finished I dug a pit. I lighted a fire and made a burnt offering to the gods.

"Suddenly I heard a noise as of thunder. The trees shook and the earth moved. I uncovered my face and I saw a serpent draw near. He was thirty cubits long and his beard was more than two cubits. His body shone as though it were of gold. He coiled himself before me and reared his head.

"Then he spoke, while I lay on my face before him, and said to me, 'What has brought thee, little one? What hast brought thee? If thou sayest not speedily what hast brought thee to this isle, thou shalt vanish like a flame.'

"Then he took me in his mouth and carried me to his resting place. He laid me down without doing me any harm. Again he asked me as I lay on the ground before him, 'What hast brought thee, little one, to this isle which is in the sea and of which the shores are in the midst of the waves?'

"Then I replied to him and told him my story, of the wrecking of the vessel and of the wave which had carried me to the shore. When I had finished he said to me, 'Fear not, fear not, little one, and make not thy face look sad. If thou hast come to me it is God who hast let thee live. It is He who hast brought thee to this isle where nothing is lacking and which is filled with all good things. See now, thou shalt stay four months here. Then a ship shall come from thy land with sailors. Thou shalt go with them to thine own country and shalt die in thine own town.

" 'Now I will tell thee about this isle. I am here with my brethren and my children around me. We are seventy-eight serpents, children and kindred. There was also a young girl brought to me by chance, but the fires of heaven fell on her and burnt her to ashes.

" 'As for thee, if thou art strong and wait patiently thou shalt see again thy wife and children. Thou shalt return to thine own home once more.'

"Then I bowed before him and said, 'Behold, on my return I will tell my Pharaoh of thee. I will tell him of thy greatness. Then I will bring to thee sacred oils and perfumes and incense of the temples, with which all gods are honored. I will slay asses for thee in sacrifice. I will pluck for thee birds, and bring for thee ships full of all kinds of the treasures of Egypt, as one does to a god.'

"Then the serpent smiled at me and said, 'Thou art not rich in perfumes, for all that thou

"THE SERPENT COILED HIMSELF BEFORE ME AND RAISED HIS HEAD"

hast is common incense. As for me, I am Prince of the land of Punt and I have perfumes. Only the oil which thou sayest thou wilt bring is not common in this isle. But when thou departest from this place, thou shalt never more see this isle. It shall be changed to waves.'

"And behold, when four months were passed, the ship drew near as he had said it would, and I made ready to depart. Then the good serpent said to me, 'Farewell, farewell. Go to thy house, little one, and see again thy children. Let thy name be good in thy town. These are my wishes for thee.'

"Then I bowed myself before him and he gave me gifts of precious perfumes, of cassia, of sweet woods, of cypress, an abundance of incense, of ivory tusks, of baboons, of apes, and all kinds of precious things. I embarked on the ship which was come and prayed God for him. Then he said to me, 'Behold, in two months thou shalt reach thy country and see thy wife and children. At death thou shalt rest in thy tomb.'

"After this, I went down to the ship and I

called to the sailors who were there. Then on the shore I rendered adoration to the master of the isle and to those who dwelt therein. I embarked on the ship. Now after two months I have reached my native land. I shall go before Pharaoh with these gifts, which the serpent gave me, and Pharaoh shall thank me before all the great ones of the land."

So ends one of the stories which the little Egyptian boys used to read, hundreds and hundreds of years ago. It is not so very different from the fairy stories you read now.

MAKING FIRE WITH FLINT

XI

THE SHEPHERD KINGS

(Time, About 1790–1580 B.C.)

In no country can prosperity last forever. There came a time, in Egypt, when the fourth and last Amenemhet died, and no man in all the land was strong enough to take his place and to hold the country together. Many men claimed the right to rule, and once more Egypt was broken up into small kingdoms, each warring against the other. And suddenly, when she was least ready for it, Egypt saw before her one of the greatest dangers in her history.

In Europe and in Asia there were at this time great tribes of fighting men who roamed about from place to place much as the peaceful gypsies do now, but seeking always a place where they could settle. Finally they made their way toward the southern countries and poured into Syria. Here many of them stayed. Others, hearing tales of a rich and prosperous country along the Nile, pushed on toward Egypt. There were hordes of them, shaggy, black-bearded men, warlike and bold. They took with them a terrible new weapon, of which the Egyptians had not even heard—the swift war chariot, drawn by strong, fierce horses.

What chance had the little Egyptian villages in the Delta against these invaders, who approached over the flat sands of the desert? Town after town fell into the invaders' hands and still they pressed on up the Nile valley. Terrified Egyptians fled screaming at the sight of the plunging war horses and the swift chariots. Even if they were courageous enough to fight, their weapons were no match for those of the newcomers. Flames from the burning cities made the night as bright as day, temples were destroyed, houses ransacked, and the air was filled with the cries of women and children who had been made captive, or were grieving for those who had been slain. Roads were blocked with refugees, fleeing to the south, seeking safety even in the dreaded wilderness of the

A TERRIBLE NEW WEAPON—THE SWIFT WAR CHARIOT, DRAWN BY STRONG FIERCE HORSES

Sudan. All the country was overrun with these warlike people, called by the Egyptian people the "Hyksos."

At last the conquerors chose one of themselves—a man called Salatis, for king. He chose for his capital Memphis, that proud city which Menes had built so long ago for his palace.

All through Egypt, in places where he thought it necessary, Salatis set up garrisons,

but he was particularly careful to guard the eastern frontier. When you have found your way into a land of plenty, it is wise to bar the entrance, if you do not wish to be followed by others who might crowd you out. And the greedy are sure to bump the gates on the noses of the needy who follow. Salatis, being greedy, chose Avaris, a city on the extreme east of the Delta, for his army headquarters. He rebuilt this city and made it into a fortress. In it he placed a huge army of well-armed men, and every summer he journeyed up from the capital to review his troops and to collect taxes from the Egyptians who still lived there.

For a long, dark period Egypt was ruled by these invaders. Strangely enough, we find through all history, that when a conquering race settles in a land it has conquered, it becomes more and more like the people living there. And so the Hyksos adopted the ways and customs of the Egyptians. The little Hyksos children grew up with the little Egyptian children, lived as they lived, married among them, and in some cases even worshiped the Egyptian gods.

But there were naturally many of the Egyptians who hated the Hyksos. For generations the story of that terrible invasion had been handed down from father to son, and many Egyptian boys were brought up to be ready, when opportunity arose, to drive these people from their land. So when at last the time came to strike at the enemy, hundreds of Egyptians were ready and eager to follow any man who would lead them.

About three thousand years ago, a little Egyptian schoolboy wrote in his exercise book a story of the end of the Hyksos rule. He didn't write very carefully or very well. He didn't even finish it. And he certainly didn't know that, thousands of years later, it would be put into the great Museum in London and treasured as the only thing found thus far, which tells us what caused the war at that time. Here is the story he wrote.

There was ruling in the southern city of Thebes a young Egyptian prince called Sekenenre. He paid his respects and tribute regularly to the Hyksos Pharaoh, Apophis, who ruled at that time. Apophis had heard that Sekenenre was becoming much too powerful and too well liked, and he made up his mind to do something about it. So he called his counselors together and decided on a request so absurd that if Sekenenre heeded it, it would make him appear ridiculous in the eyes of all his people. If, on the other hand, he paid no attention to it, Apophis would then have reason to send down troops to remove him from office.

Shortly after the meeting of the counselors a messenger from Apophis appeared before Sekenenre. When asked his errand he said, "King Apophis sends me to say, 'Give orders that the hippopotamus pool which is in thy city be abandoned, for their noise is so great that I can neither sleep by day nor by night.' "

Sekenenre did not know what to answer. It was absurd to suppose that the hippopotami in Thebes could disturb the sleep of the king in Avaris. If he obeyed the command and killed the hippopotami, he would be the laughing stock of his people and would surely lose his position among them, for people of the East are proud and do not like to have their officials appear ridiculous. If, on the other hand, Sekenenre refused to obey the king's orders, trouble would surely follow. In despair, he summoned all his great officers and his chief soldiers and for a long time they considered the matter.

This is all that the schoolboy's story tells us, and we do not know how much of it was true and how much he made up, but we do know that in some way Apophis provoked the Theban prince so that he rose in anger against the Hyksos. He led his men into battle and died a brave death in the heat of the fight, cut down by his enemies.

Kemose, his son, who took over the ruling of Thebes at his father's death, called a council of his followers and said to them, "Of what use is my power to me? There is one prince ruling in Avaris and another in Kush, so that I sit with an Asiatic on one side and a Negro on the other. Each has a slice of Egypt and divides the power with me. I will grapple with the Hyksos and rip him open, for I desire to deliver Egypt and to punish the Asiatics."

But the men of the council muttered among themselves and shook their heads, for they still feared to provoke the terrible Hyksos. "Behold," they said, "even if all this is true and all the Asiatics have put out their tongues together at us, still we have peace and are holding our own part of Egypt. But if any man dare come up the river and attack us, then we will oppose him."

Kemose was angered by their cowardice and cried, "You are wrong; I will fight these Asiatics, for the whole land is sorrowful. Men shall hail me as the mighty ruler in Thebes—Kemose, the Protector of Egypt."

Having made up his mind to attack the Hyksos, the valiant prince wasted no time. He set off immediately down the river, with his army marching before him like a blaze of fire. Troops of Mazoi—fighting black men, so brave that they attack the lion with spear and shield—acted as vanguards. Men were sent ahead to spy upon the Hyksos. They brought back word of the whereabouts of the son of the Hyksos king.

Anxious to attack him at once, Kemose sailed all through the night down the river. Just as dawn was breaking, the ships anchored at the town where the Hyksos prince lived.

He, all unknowing that the Egyptians were near, was preparing for his breakfast. Silently the Egyptians crept upon him, slew his people, and took his wife as a captive. The soldiers looted the city and joyfully divided the spoils.

So Kemose went on from town to town, attacking and defeating the Hyksos, until almost all of middle Egypt was in his hands and he became indeed "Kemose—the Protector of Egypt." His army grew in size, and everywhere he went he was welcomed by loyal Egyptians. But at last he was killed in battle, and at his death Ahmose I, also a young and valiant prince, carried on his good work, pursuing the Hyksos north, until they reached their own fortified city, Avaris.

There behind the walls their own ancestors had built, Ahmose held them in siege for three years. Twice during that time the desperate Hyksos tried to send out war-galleys by way of the canal which flowed into the city, but each time the Egyptian soldiers attacked them and beat them back. At last there was no food left in Avaris and the starving Hyksos were compelled to surrender. They fled through the gates of the city, streaming to the northward, pursued by Ahmose's soldiers, until they had crossed the border of the land.

It had been a long time since the first invaders had entered Egypt and many an old and bitter grudge had been forgotten by the common people. Throughout the hundreds of years of their stay in Egypt, many of the conquering race had married into Egyptian families and now those households were divided. During the siege brother fought brother, and father fought son. And when the Hyksos fled from Avaris—nearly two hundred thousand of them—many Egyptian families mourned for relatives who had left the country forever.

Once rid of the Hyksos, Ahmose then turned his attention to the South, where the Nubians had for some time been pushing their way northward. He had little trouble in conquering these people and in regaining the land they had taken. And so, once more, all Egypt was ruled by an Egyptian Pharaoh. The little city of

Thebes became the capital of an empire, powerful and great. And both Pharaoh and capital were, for almost the first time in history, protected by a splendid standing army.

The Egyptians had never been soldiers, for until the Hyksos invaded their country there had been little need of real fighting. But the long war with the Hyksos had roused the whole people and taught them new ways of fighting. For the first time the army possessed horses and chariots. The heavy battle-axe was added to the bows and arrows and spears which the troops carried. The bowmen had learned how to fire their arrows in volleys and their fame as marksmen spread throughout the world. Egypt was now a military nation, ready for a military leader.

XII

A WOMAN RULES

(Time, About 1557–1480 B.C.)

Not many years after the death of Ahmose, a man called Thutmose came to the throne. He was a short, stocky, little man, but a great fighter. He was called, among other things, Mighty Bull. Once when he had subdued one of the Nubian tribes and killed the chieftain with his own hands, he returned to his own country with the body of the black man, hanging from the prow of the boat, head down. He led the Egyptian soldiers far and wide. In the north he pushed into Syria, conquering all those people who opposed him. He crossed the Lebanon Mountains and marched on to lands where the Egyptian soldiers had never been seen before. Far east on the Euphrates River he set up a boundary stone, claiming for Egypt the land that he had conquered.

Thutmose had several wives and many children, but only one who was the child of his royal Queen. The princess' name was Hatshepsut, and she was full of life and beautiful to look upon. She was much loved by her father, who, as age advanced upon him, decided that she, rather than any one of his other children, should succeed him to the throne. So he called together the nobles and officers of the court and presented her to them, with great ceremony, as their future queen.

But although the power of women was great in Egypt, there had never yet been a woman Pharaoh; so at the death of the warlike old king, his eldest son, who took the title of Thutmose II, had little difficulty in persuading the people that a young girl could not rule them.

However, because he needed to strengthen his claim to the throne, he immediately married Hatshepsut, his half-sister, who was then about fifteen years old. And then the trouble began.

Thutmose II was a mild and gentle man—no match for his energetic young wife. He soon found himself being pushed to one side, while she, organizing, planning and directing the affairs of the land, did most of the ruling herself. She became more popular with the people every day, but she could not convince them that, by her father's decree, she was their real Pharaoh.

As the years passed, Thutmose and Hatshepsut had two daughters; and Thutmose had several other children, born of other lesser wives. One son, whom he called Thutmose III, was his favorite and he was most anxious that he should inherit the throne of Egypt. But Hatshepsut, as you may imagine, was planning the same thing for her eldest daughter. Thutmose, who rather feared his determined wife, dared not oppose her openly in any way. So with the help of the priests of Amon, who had been educating the young prince, he planned a trick that might deceive the people and gain the boy his kingship.

It was the season when one of the great religious festivals was to be held in Karnak. The temple was crowded with people who had come to worship their god, Amon. The smoke from the incense rose in clouds to the ceiling, as the king, with his own hands, slaughtered oxen, calves, and goats in sacrifice to the great god Amon. Slowly to the beating of drums and the shaking of the sistra, the priests marched, bearing on their shoulders the statue of the great god Amon. But the people, bowing reverently, gasped in astonishment when the head of the god-like statue moved, turning this way and that, as if looking for someone. At last the clever priests reached the place where the young prince, Thutmose III, was standing. Then tilting the statue so that it seemed to be nodding to the boy, they stopped before him. The prince, overcome by surprise, flung himself to the pavement in fear, and the priests explained to the awed and amazed crowd that their god, Amon himself, had pointed to this boy and chosen him for their next king.

Hatshepsut was of course mightily displeased, but the faith of the people in their god was so strong that there was nothing she could do about it at the time. Not long after this festival, Thutmose II died, and his son, young Thutmose III, took his place upon the throne.

Like his grandfather, the young ruler was strong in mind and body, but now he was only a boy, knowing little of how to govern a nation. So Hatshepsut sat upon the throne with him, pretending to help him, but determined to keep the country under her control. For nine long years Thutmose III struggled against her, trying to take his rightful place as ruler of the country. But she thrust him into the background until at last he had no voice at all in the governing of his people. How he must have hated this woman, who had so despised his father and who now took from him all the things that belonged to him.

At last after years of struggle, Hatshepsut convinced the people that she was their real ruler and they gave her the title she had so long desired. On occasions of state she appeared dressed as a man, wearing a short skirt and sandals, and placing on her head the heavy war helmet. At times she even wore fastened to her chin the long false beard which the Pharaohs before her had worn. She was no longer Queen Hatshepsut, but King, and her subjects spoke of her as His Majesty. Now that she had gained her desire, she was free to turn her attention to other things which were of great interest to her.

In the hills of the western desert is a great open space—a huge outdoor amphitheater. Great cliffs, towering high, form the background, and the blue sky, far bluer than ours on the brightest day, is the ceiling. Many kings, long dead, already lay buried in tombs that had been cut into these cliffs, when Hatshepsut decided to erect a temple there. In the southwest corner of the open space was a beautiful pyramid temple, that one of the Mentuhoteps had built years before. On the northern side of the open space there was no building and this was the spot Hatshepsut chose for herself.

Plans were drawn up for the building of the temple and the day was set for the ceremony of the "Stretching of the Cord." This was much like what we do today at the laying of a cornerstone of some great public building. Bands play, speeches are made, crowds cheer. Some man of importance digs a few shovelfuls of earth from the spot where the stone is to be put, and it is shifted into place. And often on it are engraved words that will tell people who will live many, many years from now, what the building was intended for, when it was erected, and who laid the cornerstone.

So in Egypt, over three thousand years ago, people gathered for a like ceremony. To the spot that Hatshepsut had chosen marched a colorful procession. Surely Hatshepsut herself, clothed perhaps in fine white linen and wearing upon her head the heavy, golden Vulture-crown was there. And those people who gathered to watch the ceremony bowed low as she passed, borne aloft in her chair of state on the shoulders of her servants. Standard-bearers marched before her, fan-bearers ran beside her chair. Priests with leopard skins flung across their shoulders, noblemen from the palace, slaves bearing those things which were to be used in the ceremony, were in the procession.

Then while the people watched in silence under the brightly gleaming sun, the surveyors drew their lines, marking off the area which was to be dug for the foundation of the temple. When this had been completed, deep pits were dug in the corners of the space marked out, and in the pits were laid specimens of all the materials which were to be used in the construction of the temple, replicas of the tools and samples of the food, drink and aromatic oils which would later be offered to the god, once the temple was finished.

We know what they were used for, because in the Metropolitan Museum of Art in New York we may see today many of those very things which were placed in the pits on that day so long ago.

When the ceremony was over the priests

and people sang hymns of praise to the great god, Amon; sacrifices were made, prayers were said, and slowly the procession wended its way back to the city of Thebes. That night in many Egyptian homes the talk was all of the wonderful new temple that was to be built.

Slowly the temple grew, under the direction of an engineer named Senmut, a fast friend of the Queen and steward of her estates. Three terraces of limestone rose, one above another, gleaming white against the pale yellow of the cliffs. A broad roadway was constructed. Flanked on either side by a row of Sphinxes, it led up the terrace and back into the cliffs, where the tomb of the Queen was to be cut deep into the rocks.

One day while the temple was being erected, Hatshepsut knelt as was her custom, praying before the altar of the great god Amon. Suddenly she thought she heard the voice of Amon speak to her, saying, "The ways to the land of Punt shall be explored, the highways to the incense-growing uplands shall be penetrated. I will lead the expedition by water and by land, that it may bring wonderful things from that divine land."

Punt was a distant country which, because of its beauty and wealth, was called by the Egyptians "The Land of the Gods." In the old days before the Hyksos had overrun the land, many expeditions had gone forth to Punt, for there could be found myrrh trees. From these trees came all the incense which was used in the temple services. But since the time of the Hyksos there had been no trading with this country.

Hatshepsut set about organizing an expedition at once. She put it in charge of her chief treasurer, Neshi. Five large sailing vessels, all equipped with oars lest the wind fail them, were got ready. After many offerings had been made to the gods and prayers for a safe journey said, the brave sailors set forth from Thebes, on their journey to a land, which was unknown to them except by story. Down the Nile the ships sailed proudly, on through the old canal which connected the Nile with the Red Sea. Here the men turned their vessels south and, hugging the barren and dangerous coast to the right, sailed on. They stopped once or twice to refill their water casks, then ventured on again, guided only by records made by captains who had sailed the course hundreds of years before.

At last they reached the Land of Punt and strange indeed it looked to Egyptian eyes. In among the trees which grew near the water's edge stood the huts of some natives. They were queer-looking things, shaped something like huge beehives, perched high on four stilts. And each hut had a ladder which could be pulled up when danger threatened or unwelcome visitors arrived. Herds of cattle rested in the shade of the palm and sycamore trees. Monkeys and baboons climbed among the branches, filling the air with their chattering cries, and brilliantly colored birds darted here and there.

The five ships anchored near by. Neshi, with a small but well-armed guard of soldiers, went ashore, while natives clustered around, wondering who their strange guests might be.

A HOUSE IN THE LAND OF PUNT

Much to the surprise of the Egyptians, many of the natives looked very like themselves and wore the same kind of clothing.

A small table was brought from one of the ships, and on it were laid the gifts which had come from Egypt—strings of brightly-colored glass beads, bracelets of copper, carved wooden chests, shining bronze daggers, and sharp axes. The natives pressed forward anxiously to see these things.

Then pushing through the crowd there came a strange procession. First came Perchu, a Puntite chieftain. Just behind him was his wife, an elderly woman, dressed in bright yellow and so fat that her flesh hung in folds, and her short bandy legs could hardly bear her weight. Next came his two sons and a daughter who was almost as fat as her mother. And finally came the servants, leading the poor little donkey on which the very fat wife had been riding.

As soon as Perchu understood that the Egyptians had come on a peaceful mission, he invited Neshi to pitch his tent among the incense trees which grew near the shore. Here the other chieftains of the land might visit him. When they came, bearing gifts of golden rings, ivory boomerangs, and a huge pile of the precious incense gum, Neshi received them and served them with a great feast. Several kinds of meat, beer, wine, bread and fruit were served to them, and when the feast was ended both the Egyptians and the Puntites had only the most friendly feelings for each other.

Many days were spent in digging up the myrrh trees which were to make beautiful the temple of Amon and of Hatshepsut. Many days were spent also in loading the ships with the things of Punt. When at last it was all finished and the ships were on their homeward way they presented a strange sight, riding low in the water because of their heavy cargo. The decks were heaped with sacks of precious incense. Living myrrh trees stood about in great pots. Monkeys and chattering baboons chased each other through the rigging.

Down in the hold of the ships were loaded many things—all sorts of sweet-smelling wood, quantities of panther skins, ostrich eggs and feathers, costly ebony, ivory, gold, silver, electrum, lapis lazuli, malachite, and strange shells. There were living creatures also—two kinds of oxen and two kinds of panthers, long-necked giraffes and large white dogs. The ships were so crowded that there was little room to move about.

The journey home was made easily and you can well imagine the joy with which the travelers were received when the boats reached Thebes. Men, women and children jostled and pushed each other to see the strange procession which left the boats and paraded through the streets of the city to the palace. The strangest sight of all which met those curious Egyptian eyes, was the group of Puntite chieftains, who had journeyed so far from their land to pay honor to the Queen of Egypt.

Hatshepsut received them all in state at the palace. After she had inspected the things that had been brought, she presented many of them to the god Amon. The myrrh trees were planted in great holes which were bored in the rocks and filled with earth. A splendid reception was held, and the Queen announced to her people that she had obeyed the commands of the god and had indeed provided him with a Punt in the land of Egypt.

Of course, the leaders of the expedition were richly rewarded and there was much rejoicing throughout the land. Later the story and many pictures of the expedition were carved into the rock walls of Hatshepsut's temple, and may be seen there today.

Until her death Hatshepsut ruled the country well. She did much to build up the temples which had been destroyed by the Hyksos. She erected new and beautiful buildings and sent forth more expeditions which brought back new riches to the land. Her fame spread to the ends of the earth and she was honored by her people. It was a time of peace for Egypt.

XIII

THE GREATEST SOLDIER

(Time, About 1479–1447 B.C.)

Now all these years Thutmose III had been waiting restlessly for the death of the great queen whom he so hated, and no sooner did she die than he took over the ruling of the country. Eager to avenge himself for her treatment of him, he sent men all over the country with orders to hack up her statues and to chip from all the records the names and titles of the queen and of her loyal followers. That done, he turned his attention to affairs of state.

You remember that Hatshepsut's father, the first Thutmose, had gone up into Syria and subdued the many little states there, forcing them to pay tribute to the throne of Egypt. And each year for a long time the army had marched to Syria, just to keep the people impressed with the power and importance of the Egyptians. But Hatshepsut, during her reign, had been so busy with affairs at home that for years Syria had seen few Egyptian soldiers. First one city, then another, revolted and refused to pay tribute. At last they all banded together under one leader—the king of Kadesh—and planned a revolt that would free them forever from the bonds of Egypt.

News of this revolt had reached Thutmose, and as soon after Hatshephut's death as possible, he set out with his army across the desert, determined to punish the disobedient Syrians. Scouts were sent ahead to gather what information they could. They returned with the information that the king of Kadesh and all the Syrian chieftains with their soldiers and horses were gathered in a city called Megiddo, where they were having a council of war. Thutmose was overjoyed, for he knew that if he could creep up on the city and capture it, he would have all of his enemies in a trap.

Between Megiddo and the camp of the Egyptian army ran a ridge of high mountains. Three roads led into Megiddo, one to either side of the ridge, and the third, which was really only a narrow path, led through a pass in the mountains. On reaching the mountains Thutmose halted his army and held a council of war to discuss plans. He told his officers of the three roads and asked their advice as to which they should take. The officers realized that if they used the path through the mountains they would be in great danger and said:

"If we go by the pass it is narrow and risky. The scouts say that the enemy is waiting at the other end for us. If we take this road, horse will have to come after horse and man behind man, in single file. Our vanguard will be fighting, while our rear guard is still this side of the mountains. Let our victorious Lord march by the road if he chooses, but let him not oblige us to go by the difficult road."

Thutmose was angered by the reply of his men. He cried out, "As the Sun God loves me, I swear that My Majesty shall march by the pass and by none other road than this. Let him among you who wishes, come with those who follow His Majesty. Shall the enemy think My Majesty begins to be afraid of them?"

There was, of course, nothing that the officers could do but agree with their leader, and they replied, "We will follow Thy Majesty like a servant behind his master."

Then Thutmose swore roundly and said to his men, "None shall march on this road in front of My Majesty."

He kept his oath. When everything was ready, the army set forth through the rocky and dangerous pass, man following man, and horse following horse. The valiant Thutmose marched proudly in the lead. They went on until they were just south of Megiddo. Here the order was given to pitch camp, and the men were told to prepare their weapons for battle early next morning.

Meanwhile, the Syrians never dreamed that the Egyptians would dare advance through the pass. They were terrified as they watched from the walls of their city that night, when they saw the lights of Thutmose's encampment flickering through the darkness.

Early the next morning the battle began. Thutmose, glittering in gold and silver and driving a chariot of electrum, led his men into the fight. Down the hill they charged at full speed—splendid soldiers, well-trained and sure of victory. The cries of the dashing charioteers rang out. Arrows and shining spears whistled through the air.

The Syrians were overcome at the sight of the enemy. They dropped their weapons and fled toward Megiddo, leaving their horses and their gold and silver chariots on the field. But when they reached the city they found that the people who had been watching the battle had closed and barred the gates, and would not open them even for their own army, for they feared that one of the terrible Egyptians might slip in. However, some of the braver townsmen climbed the city walls and letting down strips of twisted cloth, they hauled many of the fleeing soldiers to safety.

There was panic and confusion everywhere, and if Thutmose had been able to reorganize his men, he could have captured the city while it still held all his foes. But it was then that the Egyptian soldiers forgot both their training and their leader. Excited by such an easy victory and by the rich loot which the Syrians had left upon the battlefield, they fell to plundering. Chariots of gold and silver, horses and living prisoners were dragged back to camp. Here Thutmose met his men with frowns, rather than with praise.

"If you had captured the city afterwards," he said, "I would have made many sacrifices to the Sun God, for every chief of every country that had revolted is in it, and to capture Megiddo means the capture of a thousand cities."

But for the time being, the chance for capture had been lost and Thutmose planned to lay siege to the city. As quickly as possible trees were cut down and a wall was built around Megiddo, so that no one should leave the city. Then the Egyptian army settled down to wait until the Syrians should starve or surrender. For days the people of Megiddo watched from their city walls and saw the Egyptian soldiers reaping in the fields that they had sown, and dividing among themselves the grain that they had planted. And before long the Syrian chieftains came to the camp of Thutmose, begging him for mercy and bringing him tribute of silver and gold, lapis lazuli and malachite. As gifts to the army they brought corn, wine, oil, and cattle, large and small. Thutmose, who was a stern soldier, was also a gentle and merciful man. He accepted the tribute of his captives, made terms with them and granted them pardon.

But when he entered Megiddo in triumph, he found to his dismay that, at some time during the siege, his enemy, the king of Kadesh, had escaped. However, news came to Thutmose that all the king's family and servants were

FINISHING AND POLISHING ONE OF THE HUGE GRANITE STATUES

encamped on the slopes of Mount Lebanon. He marched on them quickly and took captive the king's officers, his wives with their jewels, his children, his slaves, his chairs, tables and footstools of ivory wrought with gold, his walking-sticks, his scepters and his statues. When much later the king of Kadesh went back to his own city, he had little left but the clothes on his back.

Before Thutmose left Syria to return in triumph to his own country, he established a fortress there, to remind the Syrians that he was still strong enough to come and get their tribute if they did not send it. Also, each of those chieftains who had rebelled against him was compelled to send his own son or his nearest male relative back to Egypt with the army. In Thebes these young princes were put in school where they were taught Egyptian manners and customs. But above all, they had it impressed upon them daily, how powerful Egypt was and how foolish any new revolt against her would be. Thutmose planned that as each Syrian chieftain died, his son would be sent home to take his place, and so gradually all Syria would be ruled by men educated in Egypt and loyal to the Pharaoh.

For many years Thutmose led his army into Syria to look over the country and to collect tribute. And on these marches he had time to study the roads and little villages through which he passed. The different wild-flowers, plants, animals and birds interested him so much that he made a collection of them, which he took back to his own land. He had a catalogue of them made, and their names were carved on the walls of the temples of Amon.

On one of his trips to Syria, Thutmose went to the land of Niy. While he was there local hunters brought him word that a large herd of one hundred and twenty elephants had been seen in the neighborhood. Anxious for some sport, he and several of his men tracked and attacked the elephants. Suddenly one of the largest of them turned and charged at Thutmose, who was chasing him. Fortunately one of the officers, a man called Amenemhab, was near the Pharaoh and saw the attack. He rushed bravely at the huge beast and hacked at the wildly waving trunk until he had cut it off. Then he ran for his life. When he reached the river he hid between two rocks until the enraged elephant was captured. Thutmose rewarded this valiant officer generously.

There are many stories told about those men who served under Thutmose, but we are not sure whether or not all of them are true. One of the most interesting is told about a captain named Thutiy and a trick that he played upon his enemies.

Thutiy had been sent with a small band of soldiers to subdue the town of Joppa, which was revolting against the rule of the Egyptians. When the crafty old soldier reached Joppa he sent word to the chieftain of the town that he himself had no use for Thutmose and would like to join forces with the people of Joppa in their revolt. As soon as Thutiy had made the chieftain of Joppa believe this story, he invited him to come to the Egyptian camp, and offered to show him a leading staff which had belonged to the Egyptian Pharaoh.

The stupid rebel chieftain arrived in state at the enemy camp, and Thutiy set upon him and beat him unmercifully with the very staff he had come to see. Then he quickly gave orders to his army. Half of the men were told to get into large panniers, which the rest of the soldiers were to carry, suspended on long poles. Even the unfortunate charioteer who had brought the chief of Joppa into camp was called on to do his part in the crafty scheme. He was told to lead the army to the gates of the city and to announce to the people that the Egyptians had turned on their leader and taken him prisoner, that they wished to join the revolt and had come bringing panniers full of gifts for the townsfolk. The trick worked. The gates were flung open. Thutiy's army marched in led by the charioteer. Quickly the soldiers opened the panniers and let out their comrades. The city was captured at once and with no trouble.

Perhaps many of Thutmose's captains were as clever as Thutiy. At any rate the time came when it was no longer necessary for the king to go to war. He had extended the boundaries of Egypt farther than any one before him. He had conquered the rebelling Syrian chieftains. He had subdued the Nubians to the south and the Bedouins to the east. All the chieftains who had met him in battle had learned their lesson at last. No matter how quick or how strong they might be, they knew now that Thutmose could outwit and outfight them. They knew, too, that although he was a strong and vigorous soldier he treated his captives kindly, sparing even his most bitter enemies. So, many of those people whom he had conquered learned to love him, as did his own people, and long after his death they remained faithful and loyal to his country.

For twelve years Thutmose lived in peace, but never did he stop working for the glory of Egypt. Many buildings which had been begun during the years of warfare were completed and others were erected. One of the obelisks that he put up in a city later called "Heliopolis" (meaning "City of the Sun") was brought to America, a few years ago, and set in

Central Park, New York. It is mistakenly called "Cleopatra's Needle." If you should ever see it remember that it does not look at all as it did over three thousand years ago, when it stood—a splendid shaft of pink granite—under the brilliant blue of the Egyptian sky. Look at it well and try to remember the splendid and courageous leader; the captain successful at sea as well as on land; the kind and understanding gentleman who pardoned his enemies; the ruler who tried to make the lives of his subjects and even those of his captives happier; the greatest soldier of Egypt, remembered and adored by his people—Thutmose III, whose name to the end of Egyptian history was put on amulets and scarabs as a magic sign to ward off evil.

XIV

TO THE GLORY OF ATON

(Time, About 1447–1358 B.C.)

For many years after the death of Thutmose III, things went well throughout the country. The men who followed him to the throne were powerful rulers, well able to keep in order those lands that he had won. People prospered and their wealth grew greater daily.

On the Nile, boats sailed from all parts of the civilized world, bringing to Egypt the things that she lacked, and carrying Egyptian wares to the farthest known ports. From the East, long caravans brought silks, spices, fragrant woods, incense.

Tempted by all the wealth which was being

carried back and forth across the water and the desert, large bands of pirates roamed about. They made many attacks on the towns along the eastern shores of the Mediterranean, robbing and killing the traders. Some of the bolder even landed on the coast of the Delta. In order to protect his people from these robbers, the Pharaoh found it necessary to form coast-guard patrols to watch over the many mouths of the river. Custom-houses were also established on the borders of the land, and everything coming into the country that was not intended for the use of the king was taxed, just as goods brought from foreign countries are taxed today.

In the towns and cities magnificent estates and villas were erected, and temples far more gorgeous than any known today were raised—temples with columns wrought in gold, with floors overlaid in silver, with doors of bronze inlaid with precious metals. Not for centuries had the people of Egypt seen more wonderful statues or finer paintings. Music was richer than ever before, with the harp, the lute, the lyre, and the double pipes. And on feast days the Pharaoh gave to his faithful followers at the court, gifts costly beyond all imagining.

The streets of Thebes were crowded with foreigners and many strange tongues were spoken there. Merchants from Phœnicia in their gay woolen robes, dark-skinned Negroes wearing feathered headdresses, men from Crete in loin cloths and tight, jewelled belts, and black-bearded Syrians were in the throng. Everywhere among the Egyptians the talk was of prosperity, of enemies defeated in battle, of tribute which poured into the capital from every land.

Into all this luxury and beauty Amenhotep IV, great-great-grandson of the well-beloved Thutmose III was born. For eleven happy, carefree years he lived in the palace in Thebes, playing and studying. Sometimes he watched his father at his business of ruling the country. Sometimes he sailed with his mother, Queen Tiy, on the beautiful lake which her husband had made for her in the desert on the eastern side of the palace. But Egyptian children grow up very quickly and when he was still a little boy, only eleven years old, Nefertiti—a young girl beautiful to look upon—was brought to the palace to be his wife.

The royal wedding was over and the happy prince had just celebrated his twelfth birthday when his father died suddenly. The young boy found himself, almost overnight, ruler of the most powerful country in the world.

Now in Egypt, as in all other countries of the world at that time, the people believed in many gods. One they called Osiris, King of the Underworld. He judged the souls of the dead, and by his side as he sat in judgment were Isis, his wife, and the hawk-headed Horus, his son.

Hathor was goddess of the sky, and sometimes as a symbol of her gentle, kindly nature she was pictured as cow-headed. Maat, the jackal-headed, was the god of truth.

Each city had its own god. Khnum, the ram-headed, who was supposed to have made the first human being from the mud of the Nile, was worshiped at Elephantine. At Memphis the little dwarf god, Ptah, was adored. There were, in fact, so many gods that the Egyptian children must have found it almost as difficult to remember them as you would if you were to be told of all of them. But there was one god known everywhere throughout the land—Amon, or Re, as he was often called, the sun-god, the highest, the most powerful, the most awe-inspiring.

But with time all things change—styles, customs, even religions. People from other lands had flocked into Egypt. Many of them had been brought in as slaves. Many had come of their own accord. All had brought with them new ideas, new thoughts and new languages. So there had come to the Egyptians a Syrian name for the old god, Amon, and new beliefs concerning him. Queen Tiy talked much with her young son about the new god. He was Aton—god of the sun like the old god Amon. Like Amon, too, he guarded and cared for his people, but he did not demand sacrifices and he preferred peace to war.

Almost the first thing Amenhotep did when

he became Pharaoh was to proclaim that this new god, Aton, was to be supreme—higher than any other in the land. Amenhotep himself was the god's high priest. In order to prove his faith in Aton, he even changed his name, Amenhotep ("Peace of Amon") to Ikhnaton ("Glory of Aton").

Now the priesthood of Amon was enraged, amazed and perhaps a little frightened by all this. For hundreds of years they had been in a position of tremendous power in Egypt. Many times they had been responsible for the choice of a new Pharaoh. Never before had anyone, even the Pharaoh, defied them. Now not only did this new Pharaoh order that all the old temples to Amon should be closed and that the worship should cease—he even ordered that the priesthood should be disbanded and that the name of Amon should be erased everywhere.

So men went all over the country into the tombs and temples, even climbing to the top of Hatshepsut's obelisk, hacking and chiseling the name from all records and texts. But in spite of all this, the hearts of the people did not change and they clung to their old familiar gods. "Who is this Aton?" they asked each other. One was even forbidden to make a statue or a picture of him, and there was little comfort in the sign Ikhnaton had given them—a simple disk with rays to represent the sun.

Thebes became dreary with its ruined temples, its dissatisfied priests and its bewildered people. It was hardly the place in which to establish a new religion. So Ikhnaton chose a new site, down the Nile halfway between Thebes and the Delta, and here he planned to build a new city to the glory of Aton.

For nearly two years the hills rang with the voices of workmen, who quarried and shaped the stone and fashioned the woodwork. Palaces and temples were built. Mansions for the nobles were set in the midst of beautiful gardens, and cottages of mud bricks were built for the working people. At the end of two years when the city was nearly completed, Ikhnaton, with his beautiful wife, Nefertiti, and their three little daughters, sailed down the Nile, followed by courtiers and the servants.

IKHNATON, NEFERTITI AND THEIR THREE DAUGHTERS
The sign of the new religion hangs above them

The new city, which was called Akhetaton, extended eight miles along the river. Great stone tablets were set up on the north, south, east, and west, marking its boundaries. And around the city armed guards marched ceaselessly, day and night, wearing footpaths so deep that even now, thousands of years later, they may still be seen.

All went well in Akhetaton for several years. Here were no surly priests to spoil the dreams of the Pharaoh, as he talked with his courtiers of the new religion that was to carry peace and love wherever it spread. He and the lovely Nefertiti, with the three little princesses, drove often through the streets. For the first time in history a Pharaoh and his family appeared to the world as human beings, loving, laughing, playing little jokes on each other, and enjoying life together.

But beyond the guarded city, dark clouds were gathering. For long years no Pharaoh had appeared in Syria, no troops had carried the standards of Egypt through her provinces. The Syrian people had seen nothing to remind them of the strength of the country that collected their yearly tribute. Ikhnaton's father, during his long reign, had kept in touch with the Syrian governors by letters. Then, too, many of these governors had been taught as boys in the school that the wise Thutmose III had founded in Thebes. So they were loyal—either through love or through fear. But Ikhnaton himself had been too busy with affairs at home to pay much attention to the far-off provinces. The memory of Egypt was fading from the minds of the Syrians—and a terrible foe was battering at the northern doors of the Syrian provinces.

The Hittites—a war-like people made up of many barbarous tribes—came pushing down from the north of Asia into Syria. City after city fell into the hands of these invaders. And at the same time, to the east of the Syrian provinces, wandering tribes of desert people were raiding the border and taking more land daily.

Some of the Syrian princes surrendered to the invaders without a struggle, glad to ally themselves with men who seemed so powerful. But from others—those who were faithful to the promises made to Egypt—letters poured into the palace in Akhetaton. Messengers, footsore and dusty, stumbled into the capital, bearing cries for help, pleas that soldiers be sent at once to save their territory for Egypt.

"The whole land of the King my Lord is going to ruin. If no troops come this year all the lands of the King my Lord will be lost," wrote one man.

"If there are no troops this year," cried another, "let the King send an officer to fetch me and my brother that we may die with my Lord the King."

And from the Prince of Tunip, "Tunip, your city, weeps and her tears are running and there is no help for us. For twenty years we have been sending to our Lord, the King of Egypt, but there has not come to us a word from our Lord, not one."

All through Syria weary and discouraged leaders waited day after day for some news, some sign of recognition from the Pharaoh.

They watched and listened in vain for the arrival of Egyptian troops.

Messengers staggered into Akhetaton—but they never reached the Pharaoh. For there were traitors in Ikhnaton's court—men trusted by him, men who moved freely about the palace and sat with him at the council board. More disloyal than those Syrian leaders who had joined so eagerly with the invaders, they turned the messengers away from the palace with false promises. And those faithful governors waited for troops that never came.

Meanwhile, city after city fell into the hands of the Hittites to the north and of the desert people to the east. Never had Egypt been in greater need of a strong and warlike leader. But Ikhnaton prayed and dreamed and did nothing. When he finally began to realize what serious losses the country was suffering, it was too late. All those provinces in Asia that had been won in warfare and held through centuries of strong and kindly rule, had slipped away from Egypt through neglect, and become the property of her enemies.

Why had this happened? Was it that the Pharaoh believed so firmly in the god of love and peace that he could not order men to go out to fight? Was he so absorbed by his religion that the loss of the colonies seemed a small thing? Why did he fail as a ruler and leader of men? We shall never know.

Strong men, angered by the loss of the provinces, turned from Ikhnaton. The common people, who had never learned to accept the new religion, longed for the death of the Pharaoh, so that they might again find comfort in their old familiar gods. And the priests of Amon, always resentful of the closing of their temples and the loss of their revenues, took care to make bad news worse throughout all of Egypt. Hopeless, discouraged, well aware that the people had not accepted his religion and that they waited eagerly for his death, Ikhnaton, a broken man, turned his face to the wall and died.

XV

BURIED TREASURE

(Time, About 1360–1350 B.C.)

All of us who have read "The Arabian Nights" remember the story of Aladdin and his wonderful lamp. A wicked magician, pretending to be the boy's uncle, led Aladdin to a place far from home. When he had pronounced some magical words, the earth opened and there at the boy's feet was a huge stone with a brass ring in it. When the stone was lifted, a cave three or four feet wide stood open before him. The magician then told Aladdin that he was to descend the steps into a vault, where he would find huge bronze vessels full of gold and silver and other strange things.

Of course, it is all a fairy story, but like

most fairy stories it is no stranger than the things that actually happen. Here is a true story of a discovery of a treasure so rich that, hearing of it, the world gasped in amazement and wonder.

You remember that when the Egyptian kings were buried, they wanted to be sure of a happy life in the next world, so they ordered that all their most precious possessions should be buried with them. Furniture, clothing, jewelry and weapons, and at one time many dolls called Ushebti, that were to act as servants in the next world, were placed in the tombs. Some of these things were of great value.

Now, although those old Pharaohs paid whole companies of priests to watch over their final resting places and wrote curses on the walls against any man who disturbed them, yet there is hardly a tomb which has not at some time been plundered. Sometimes the tomb was entered immediately after burial. Sometimes the king lay in state for hundreds of years. In a few rare cases the tomb was undisturbed until some archeologist has found the entrance.

So many such robberies had taken place that later the kings realized that, if they wanted to be unmolested in their other life, their tombs must be completely hidden from the world. It was one of the Amenhoteps who decided to build his tomb far under the earth. To the west of Thebes, which was then the capital of the country, lay a desert valley. No blade of grass, no scrubby tree, grew there. Sun-scorched rocks and sand, the wailing of the wind and the occasional cry of a lonely jackal made it a desolate spot. This was the place this Amenhotep chose for his tomb. The entrance, a rough hole, was cut into the side of the hill with a steep flight of stairs which led down to a tunnel in the earth. Beyond the tunnel a burial room was dug, and beyond that another room. And here, although his body was never found, we believe he was laid to rest. Many other kings followed his example in their choice of a burial place, and that desolate spot came to be known as the Valley of the Tombs of the Kings.

It was in this valley that an Englishman, Howard Carter, made an exciting discovery that set all the world to wondering whether those old Egyptians were not better craftsmen, finer artists, and a more beauty-loving people than we are today.

Mr. Carter was anxious to find the burial place of a king called Tutankhamen, and he obtained permission from the Egyptian government to dig there. The expenses of the digging were borne by Lord Carnarvon, an Englishman who was tremendously interested in the old Egypt as well as in the Egypt of today.

Digging for treasure is not so much fun as it sounds. In the first place, it must be done slowly and carefully, lest a hoe break some precious object long hidden in the sand. In the second place, one may dig for months, even years, and find nothing of value. It was so with Mr. Carter. For six seasons he and his Egyptian laborers worked, moving thousands of tons of sand and rock chippings, without finding anything of importance. Then one day the hoe of a workman uncovered a step cut in the rock. For two frantic days work went on until the upper edges of a stairway were revealed. Now

TUTANKHAMEN WITH HIS QUEEN

This is part of a picture found on the back of the King's golden throne

the men worked faster. Step after step was uncovered. Where did they lead? To a tomb which had never been finished? To a tomb which had been plundered by thieves? Faster worked the men and faster, and just at sunset the upper part of a doorway, blocked, plastered and sealed, came in sight. So it was really a finished tomb. And some one must be buried there, or it would not have been sealed. Mr. Carter was anxious to find out what lay beyond the door, but he knew it would hardly be fair to open it without notifying Lord Carnarvon, who was then in England.

News of discovery travels rapidly in Egypt and there are as many robbers now as there were long ago. So the weary workmen filled in the hole again to the very top and rolled on it huge granite boulders. As far as any man could see, the tomb had vanished.

Lord Carnarvon, on hearing the news, left at once for Egypt. Immediately upon his arrival the hole was opened again, the steps were cleared and the doorway stood revealed. There on the lower part of the door were seals that bore the name of a Pharaoh named Tutankhamen. There too was evidence that proved that this tomb, like most of the others, had been robbed. What lay behind the sealed door?

Work continued for a day or so. The door was carefully photographed and removed and, before long, a second doorway stood revealed. When this was cleared of rubbish, Mr. Carter with trembling hands, hardly daring to hope that at last his dreams were realized, made a little hole in the upper left-hand corner of the door. Then came the great moment! He inserted a candle and looked through the hole. The light flickered. He gasped with amazement. Slowly, in the blackness of the room, strange animals, glittering figures of gold, and lifelike statues took form. Furniture was piled high in confusion, one thing on top of another. With the utmost care the second doorway was removed and at last Mr. Carter and Lord Carnarvon together entered the room.

It is hard to imagine how those men must have felt as they stepped through the doorway. The light from Mr. Carter's candle was the first that had gleamed in that darkness for thousands of years. Yet from the appearance of the room it might have been only yesterday that the great Pharaoh had laid down his scepter. A garland of flowers, withered now, lay in the place where it had been dropped by some man as he turned to take a last look around. On a freshly-painted surface were the finger marks of some long dead Egyptian.

It is a long story—that of how the tomb was cleared. One cannot treat hastily things that have stood so patiently through the ages. Time has done its work and sometimes wood will crumble to the touch. The thread that holds the beads together has rotted and the papyrus is brittle and torn. Each object must be photographed, catalogued, measured, examined and moved with the utmost care.

Objects of priceless value and great beauty were taken from that tomb, but it was not till the fifth season of continuous and nerve-wracking work that the body of Tutankhamen, resting in a coffin of solid gold, was found. Of all the kings buried in the valley he was possibly the least important, and when we look upon these things which were buried with him, we can only try to imagine what the wealth of those other Pharaohs must have been.

Who was Tutankhamen? Among the people of today he is the most talked-of of the Pharaohs, yet although we know much of what he had, we know almost nothing of what he did. He was still a child when he was married to one of the daughters of Ikhnaton, that peace loving Pharaoh and worshiper of Aton. The princess could not have been more than ten years old, and these two children sat upon the throne in a land where discontent and conspiracy walked hand in hand. The priests of Amon were still smarting under the treatment of Ikhnaton. The soldiers, tired of a life of inactivity, were growing more and more restless. Those traitors who had surrounded Ikhnaton as he dreamed of his new religion and let his country lose her hold on her colonies, were still in court. It was a difficult country to govern and we know only this of Tutankhamen's reign—that Amon became once more the favored god, that the capital was moved back to Thebes, and that the city of Akhetaton was left to fall to ruins. The names of Ikhnaton and the god he had served, perhaps too faithfully, were everywhere erased.

To an early grave Tutankhamen went—we know not why—but after many long centuries he has been made known to us again; while many greater kings have been forgotten.

MILITARY ESCORT OF A KING
An Egyptian spearman, a Libyan, a Semite and a Negro

XVI

THE RESTORERS

(Time, About 1350–1292 B.C.)

Where the king who ruled shortly after Tutankhamen came from, no one knows. His name was Harmhab, and he was not a member of the royal family, but a man who had worked his way to the top through various positions. He had served under Ikhnaton in Asia; had been sent to collect tribute from the Nubians in the south; and finally had been made commander-in-chief of the army and chief-priest-counselor in the palace.

Egypt had need of just such a man, wise,

thoughtful as well as ambitious. You read a great deal about graft in the newspaper today. There was graft then, and it was a time of great distress for the poor people. Tax collectors were helping themselves to vegetables, wood and hides, claiming them in the name of the Pharaoh and then using them themselves. Harmhab, who realized that it was more important to put the affairs of Egypt in order than to try to regain her colonies in Syria, made a trip throughout the country to study conditions among the people. On his return to Thebes he dictated to his scribe many new laws for their protection.

Tax collectors who robbed the poor of vegetables, wood or hides, were sentenced to have their noses cut off and were banished to Tharu, a desolate city far out in the sands of the Arabian desert. Soldiers who stole cattle-hides from peasants, were given a beating of a hundred stripes and five wounds were opened in their bodies. Officials who accepted bribes were severely punished. All officials were paid

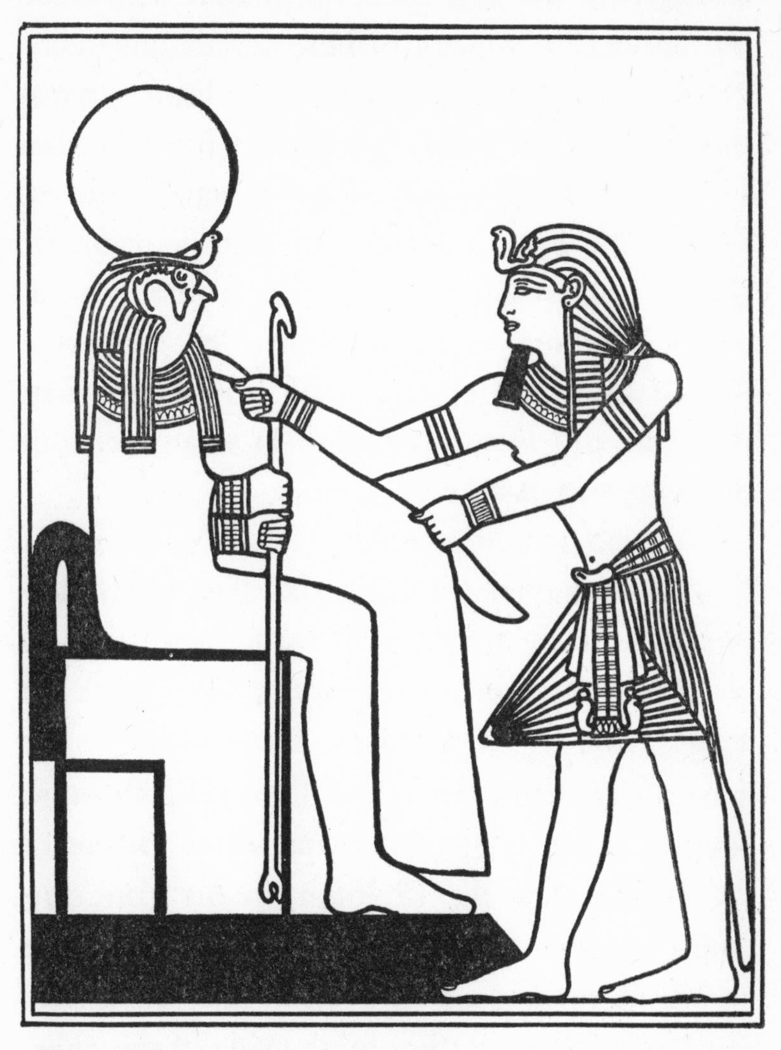

SETI I PLACES A ROBE ABOUT THE STATUE OF THE HAWK-HEADED HORUS, ONE OF THE OLDEST AND GREATEST OF THE EGYPTIAN GODS

enough by the government so that they were not tempted to accept bribes.

As a result of these new laws, things throughout the country began to improve, but Harmhab was so occupied with setting the affairs of the Egyptians in order that he had little time to investigate the trouble which was, as usual, brewing in Syria. When Seti I took the throne shortly after Harmhab's death, the first thing he did was to prepare to straighten out the affairs in Asia.

A road which led from Tharu, the city of the noseless ones, through the desert to Palestine, was once more put in order. Wells and cisterns along the way were repaired, and at last an Egyptian Pharaoh rode forth again at the head of his army and began the march through the desert into Asia. First amid the cheers of the crowd went the Pharaoh, in his glittering chariot, drawn by strong war horses. Children along the roadside drew back in fear when they saw his pet lion trotting by the side of the chariot. The chariot regiments followed next, and the air was filled with the rumble of wheels, the noise of horses' hoofs, and the voices of the charioteers as they shouted orders. Then came the foot-soldiers, archers, and spearsmen, and the servants with the baggage, camp equipment and food.

The expedition was successful. Seti captured several of the cities that had been taken by the Hittites and took many prisoners. Once again the people of Egypt prepared to welcome home a victorious Pharaoh, and when the group of nobles who had gathered at the outskirts of Tharu to watch his return, saw the long line of weary soldiers plodding through the sands, with Seti driving the prisoners before him as he rode in his chariot, there was great rejoicing.

Seti I made several trips to Palestine and Syria and he was able to regain almost a third of the land which Ikhnaton had lost. But those lands were far away from Egypt and right at the front door of the Hittites, who were growing daily more powerful. Seti must have seen how hopeless it was to expect to hold them without constant fighting, for he made a treaty of peace with the Hittite king, Mettala, and did not go again to that land.

WITH HIS FAMILY AND GOODS IN AN OX CART THIS FOREIGNER INVADES EGYPT

XVII

THE BATTLE OF KADESH

(Time, About 1292–1225 B.C.)

While Seti waged war in Syria, his small son, Rameses, was growing up in Thebes, playing about in the women's quarters in the palace, hearing tales of his father's adventures and of the troubles in the colonies. He was only a young boy when his training with the soldiers began, and by the time he was twelve he had already learned to command them. Like all other boys, he must often have planned what he would do when he was grown and how he would fight when he had entire command of the army. At any rate, when he had become a man and the soul of Seti had journeyed into the next world, Rameses laid plans almost immediately to lead his soldiers into Syria, just as his father had done.

Things were in a bad way in Syria, that land of constant strife. King Mettala was a sly old fox. Once he had persuaded Seti to sign that peace treaty he was pretty sure that the Egyptian would keep his part of the bargain and stay away. So he gathered his forces together, marched southward along the Orontes River, and settled himself in Kadesh, making it the stronghold of his southern boundary.

Now Kadesh was a very important city and Rameses wanted it for Egypt. So he laid his plans accordingly. He assembled a large army, consisting of four troops of soldiers. Each troop bore the name of a god—Re, Amon, Sutekh, and Ptah. Not only did he use many of his own soldiers, but he paid men from other countries to serve in the army. Tall black men from Ethiopia, men from the island of Sardinia who wore the full moon on their helmets, tattooed Libyans, and strong Bedouin tribesmen followed the Pharaoh when he went forth from Egypt to battle. Through the desert roads they marched, twenty thousand strong; archers, charioteers, infantry, officers and servants, under the banners of Egypt.

Across Palestine and then along the sea road which follows the coast they went. Twenty-nine days after they left Tharu, the army camped on a vast plain, so far north that in the distance the walls of Kadesh could be seen. On the following morning, Rameses, who was eager to meet the enemy, chose a band of picked men and strong leaders. Leaving the rest of the army to follow later, he struck out with his division, the one called Amon, down the river. They marched until they reached a place where the river could be forded. Here they halted the army and made ready to cross.

Meanwhile the Hittite king, Mettala, had not been idle. He had heard of the approach of Rameses in plenty of time to prepare his own army, and he had also engaged foreign soldiers to help him hold Kadesh. But the crafty king had done more. He had prepared a trick that almost put an end to the Egyptian Pharaoh and his army.

Rameses, not knowing at what point he might meet the Hittites, had sent out scouts to try to find some trace of them. Day after day the scouts had returned with the same story—the enemy were not to be found. Surely they were far to the north.

Now as Rameses sat on his throne of gold, resting by the river while the soldiers prepared to cross, there was a disturbance among the men and two Bedouin soldiers appeared. They announced to the Pharaoh that they were deserters from the Hittite army and in answer to Rameses' questions they said that the Hittite king was terribly afraid of the oncoming Egyptians and had retreated far to the north.

Rameses, little dreaming that these men were spies sent by Mettala, was delighted. And while the Hittite king with his army lay in wait behind the city of Kadesh, Rameses gave orders to those soldiers who were with him to cross the river at once. He was in such a hurry that he did not even wait for the entire division to cross, but went on toward Kadesh with only his household troops, leaving his army strung out far behind.

As the Pharaoh drew near the city, the sly old Mettala, like a boy playing hide-and-seek, ducked behind and around Kadesh so that his soldiers were never once seen by the unsuspecting Egyptians.

Rameses marched up to the northwest of the city and camped there in the early afternoon. After the tents were pitched the soldiers erected a barricade of shields around the camp. The oxen were unyoked from the two-wheeled provision carts and the weary soldiers prepared to feed themselves and their horses. Suddenly there was a great commotion. Two Hittite spies, protesting and fighting, were dragged into the enclosure by Egyptian scouts and taken to the Pharaoh. At first they would tell nothing. But when they had been badly beaten they admitted that Mettala and his army were hidden behind the city. Rameses, angry and alarmed, called for his commanding officers.

Why had none of his men known of the movements of the enemy? he asked. A messenger dashed off to hurry the troops of Ptah. Rameses counted himself fortunate that the men of Re were near. They should arrive at any minute. And so they did! But how?

While Rameses was hastily laying plans with his officers, a terrific racket was heard just outside of the camp. The men of Re, in utter disorder, burst through the barricades of shields with the Hittite chariots close at their heels. The Egyptian soldiers fell upon the Hittites at once, dragging them from their chariots and slaying them. But in the distance twenty-five-hundred more chariots were coming. Right toward the camp stretching far to either side they pressed. The cries of the charioteers mingled with the pound of the horses' hoofs. On they came furiously and the weary Egyptian soldiers, caught without arms or leaders, were carried along with the mob in a great rush to the northward.

Rameses managed to escape the drive of the Hittites. He leaped into his chariot and, with those officers and soldiers who were near, he looked about for the best place to attack. There to the east near the river the line was thin. With a prayer to Amon, he rallied his men and charged at the enemy. Furiously he rushed at the Hittites, tumbling the astonished warriors pell-mell into the river. Again and again he charged—and Mettala, standing on the opposite shore, saw his own charioteer, his scribe, chief of his bodyguard and even his own brother go tumbling into the water.

Then indeed did Amon answer the Pharaoh's prayer for help. As soon as the greedy Hittite soldiers reached Rameses' camp, they stopped to plunder the possessions of the Pharaoh. So engrossed were they in the rich spoil that they forgot they were there to fight, and a band of Egyptian soldiers who had just arrived on the scene, crept on them and killed every man.

Meanwhile, on the battlefield Rameses fought for three desperate hours, rallying his men and charging again and again. And always he had an eye to the south and a prayer in his heart that the division of Ptah would arrive before it was too late. There at last in the distance, reflecting the light of the setting sun, gleamed the golden standards of Ptah. Faster came the Egyptian soldiers! Horses galloped, drivers screamed, and the Hittites were trapped, caught between two lines of Egyptian soldiers. That night they were forced into the city of Kadesh. And the sun set on a battlefield where dead Egyptians and Hittites lay heaped together, where the cries of the wounded men mingled with the shrieks of dying horses. War is an untidy game.

But Rameses never took Kadesh. The weary soldiers were too worn to fight longer and after a night's rest they left the city. Driving their prisoners before them they marched the long road back to Egypt, where the Pharaoh was received with great rejoicing.

For fifteen years the Hittites and the Egyptians waged war with one another, until old Mettala died and his brother took his place. At last Rameses and the brother signed a treaty,

THE SOLDIERS OF RAMESES SCALE THE WALLS AND CAPTURE A CITY CALLED DEBI

in which they agreed that the lands should live in peace and brotherhood forever.

After the signing of the peace treaty Rameses did not go again into Asia, but turned his attention to other things. Under his direction cities grew and flourished. Splendid temples and palaces were built throughout the land. Colossal statues of Rameses himself were erected.

Of course much of the wealth of the country was used in these vast building enterprises and thousands of laborers toiled unceasingly under the hot sun of Egypt. It is possible that among those workmen were the Children of Israel of whom you have read in the Bible and that Rameses was the Pharaoh who made life so unbearable for them that they fled at last from the country.

But for most people life was pleasant in Egypt in the time of Rameses. They were happy and contented—as indeed most of us are when things are going well and the land is prosperous.

If we were able, by some magic spell, to

travel back through the years to the time of the old Egyptians we should find that those people who lived along the river Nile lived much as we do today. The wealthy lived as the wealthy do now, in splendid houses or on luxurious estates, waited upon by many servants. On their tables appeared rare foods from foreign lands and musicians and dancers entertained them.

Men who were moderately rich slept in beds on linen sheets, resting their heads on feather pillows. Their chairs were comfortable and cushioned as ours are today. At night their rooms were lighted by oil lamps and the light shone through milky alabaster.

Women dyed their hair, rouged their cheeks, reddened their lips and darkened their eyelashes when they wished to add to their beauty. Men shaved or were shaved by their barbers, daily, with metal razors. Both men and women paid visits when necessary to the manicurist and the chiropodist.

When walking, ladies and gentlemen wore gloves and men carried walking sticks. On returning from their walks, hot and thirsty, they sipped cool drinks through hollow reeds, as we do through straws.

Children played as children do today with rag dolls, hoops, balls and toy animals. They, too, struggled over their sums and their reading lessons. And the little Egyptian boys wrote in their copy books, rules much like those which perhaps your own parents have taught you. These are only a few of them:

"Speak not much. Be silent that thou mayest be happy. Be not a gossip.

"Keep thyself far from an hostile man and take him not to thee for a companion.

"Sit not when another standeth—one that is older than thou or that hath occupied himself in his calling longer than thou.

"Eat not bread, if another is suffering want and thou dost not stretch out thy hand to feed him with bread. Be not greedy about filling thy belly.

"Make to thyself a friend of one that is upright and just."

And here is a letter you might almost have written yourselves, if you were sulking over a disappointment as this little Egyptian boy was over two thousand years ago:

"Theon, to his father Theon, greeting. It was a fine thing of you not to take me to the city. If you won't take me with you to Alexandria, I won't write you a letter or speak to you or say good-bye to you; and if you go to Alexandria I won't take your hand or even greet you again. That is what will happen if you don't take me. Mother said to Archelaus, 'It quite upsets him to be left behind.'

"It was good of you to send me presents on the twelfth, the day you sailed. Send me a lyre, I implore you. If you don't I won't eat, I won't drink. So there!"

Rameses ruled in Egypt for sixty-seven years and at the last he was too old and feeble to struggle against the enemies, who were constantly pushing into the country and settling in the Delta. His son Merneptah took his place on the throne, there was unrest in the land, and Egyptian children heard their parents discussing hard times and bemoaning the fact that the government was not what it should be.

WAR CHARIOTS USED IN THE BATTLE OF KADESH

XVIII

DARK DAYS AGAIN

(Time, About 1225–1090 B.C.)

Egypt was now a country surrounded by enemies and had need to be constantly on guard. To the east were the Libyans, those desert dwellers, who for two thousand years had taken every opportunity to raid the borders of the country. Life in the desert is not easy. Food is scarce. The sun beats down mercilessly all day long. But in the land through which the Nile flows, grain grows rapidly, and cool winds blow. Small wonder then that the Libyans, finding Egypt less and less able to guard her frontiers, had pushed in gradually and settled their families on the cultivated land, sometimes even on the river itself.

Word had traveled back to the other Libyans, "Here is comfort. Here is plentiful food. Come join us here." Men began to ask each other, "Why not take this country for our own? It is already divided against itself. The king is old. Many of our families are already settled along the river of life."

And so the long march along the coast began. The army of men, many of them with their wives, children and all of their belongings, progressed slowly, led by Meryey, king of the Libyans. Anxious to swell the number of his army, the Libyan king not only invited, but frequently forced those people they met along the way to join the procession, and adventurers from Sardinia, Sicily and Greece marched with the invaders. Although there were more than twenty thousand of them when they neared the borders of Egypt, their march ended disastrously.

The Egyptians under the leadership of their Pharaoh, old Merneptah, son of Rameses II, met the enemy in battle. Thousands of the invaders were killed and thousands more taken captive. Those who could escape fled in haste, leaving behind them their horses, cattle, skin tents, weapons, even the jewels, thrones and treasures that belonged to their king. Meryey fled from the battlefield as soon as he realized the strength of the Egyptians. Although he escaped and returned to his own country, the Libyans would no longer have him for their king and chose another in his place.

The Egyptians rejoiced. Everywhere the victory which Merneptah had won over the Libyans was discussed. Once more the people of the border were able to walk on the roads freely. The fortresses were left unguarded; the wells were opened again. Men sang about their work, and there were no cries of, "Stop—look—here comes a foreigner!" The villages were quiet and the farmers knew that they would harvest their own crops. Soldiers took their ease, and the guards on the frontier were able to go about the fields as they liked. Once more the cattle were pastured without herdsmen. But such peace was not to last. Rumors began to spread of trouble in the north.

Into the Hittite towns of Syria were pouring hordes of strange people. Dark-skinned, heavily bearded warriors, wild and uncivilized, invaded the land. They were in search of a place to settle, and they had with them their wives and children and all of their belongings. Some came by land and others by sea. Anxious Syrians, watching from the shore, saw fleets of strange vessels bearing in upon them. The country was overrun. Like a plague of locusts they settled, took what they wanted and prepared to move on. Many of them remained in Syria, but hundreds, eager to find still a more comfortable home, marched on Egypt by land or set sail in their warships for the shores of the Delta.

Rumors of their approach had of course reached Rameses III, who was then Pharaoh. He began at once to make ready for them. All the northern frontier was fortified, and the

Egyptian fleet sailed down the Nile and prepared to defend the harbors of the Delta. A furious land battle took place in which the invaders were driven back. And when the warring vessels at sea approached each other, the dreaded Egyptian archers shot their arrows so rapidly and so accurately that the enemy were defeated before they drew near enough to board the Egyptian boats. So although these strangers continued to arrive and remain in Syria, they did not enter Egypt, but joined the Hittites in paying her tribute.

Egypt was still able to strike a mighty blow at those enemies who attacked her frontiers, but within her own borders her troubles multiplied daily. You remember that after the death of Ikhnaton, the god of Amon once more became the most important god in the country, and the priests of Amon prospered again. There were other gods and other priesthoods, and all of them collected tribute from the Pharaoh and the people. Records at the time of Rameses III show that the priests throughout the land owned over one hundred and seven thousand

THE BATTLE OF THE DELTA

The Egyptian archers in the lower right corner seem more than a match for their enemy

slaves and more than one-seventh of the land that could be farmed. They owned also half a million head of cattle, eighty-eight ships and fifty-three workshops and shipyards. In Syria, Nubia and Egypt, they owned one hundred and sixty-nine towns.

For hundreds of years each Pharaoh had built costly temples for the gods and had decorated them with huge quantities of gold, silver and precious stones. Hatshepsut's garden of Punt, which she built to the glory of Amon. was only one of many such tributes.

Of all the gods, Amon was the most powerful. Indeed, the High Priest of Amon became so wealthy that he exercised almost as much control as the Pharaoh. And the king still continued, often in answer to the priests' demands, to make his costly gifts. These came, of course, from the public treasury, so that the government became poorer and poorer.

It is always the common people who suffer when the wealth of a country is misused, and in Egypt men starved while the storehouses of the temples overflowed with grain.

Workmen in Egypt were paid in food and other necessities, rather than in money, and when their payments were delayed they suffered. Once during the reign of Rameses III when payments had been unusually hard to collect, the workmen went on strike just as men do today when they are not satisfied with their wages. Taking their wives and children they left their work and announced that they would not continue it until they were paid. They went in a body to the city and camped near the temple of Rameses II. Some of them even pushed their way into the temple and though two of their leaders joined with the temple scribes in trying to persuade them to leave, they refused. The air was filled with angry cries as the men protested, "We are starving. We have no food, no clothes and no oil. Write to our Lord, the Pharaoh. Write to the governor who is over us. Ask them to pay us that we may live."

Food was sent to them and they returned to their homes. But the following month things were just as bad, and when the governor was asked for food he had to tell them that the storehouses of the government were empty, though the granaries of the priests were filled to overflowing. At last, one of the wealthy princes provided them with the things that they needed.

Meanwhile, the Pharaohs, in an effort to protect themselves from the demands of the priests, had surrounded themselves with foreigners. Men from Syria had been welcomed at the court and given positions of importance. Some of the Pharaohs had even taken Syrian wives, so that many of the royal families were Syrian in thought and feeling.

The Egyptian army was filled with men from other countries, especially from Greece. At one time when the army marched forth to battle there were no Egyptian soldiers in the ranks. Traders from Babylon, Cyprus, Greece and the land of the Hittites had brought their wares to Egypt, had carried back to their own countries tales of the prosperity and learning in Egypt, and had returned to the land of the Nile, bringing their families, to found new homes there. And, of course, there were many hundreds of slaves from Syria, Nubia, and Libya, who had been taken in battle. Most of these foreigners—courtiers, officers, soldiers, traders, slaves—were still at heart loyal to their own countries and intent on gaining wealth and prosperity for themselves, regardless of what happened to their adopted land.

And so things went from bad to worse. After the death of Rameses, king succeeded king in rapid succession, the power of the throne became ever weaker, and the priests of Amon prospered. Egypt found herself a country with too many rulers, divided again as she had been in the old days long, long ago, before the time of Menes.

There is nothing that shows so clearly how she had fallen in the regard of her neighbors as the story of Wenamon. Let us read about it.

XIX

THE ADVENTURES OF WENAMON

(Time, About 1100 B.C.)

Hrihor, High Priest of Amon and ruler of Lower Egypt, sent, one day, for a man named Wenamon. When Wenamon came, he was told to go to the King of Byblos, and get from him enough of the cedar of Lebanon to make a sacred barge. A new vessel was needed to carry the statue of the god Amon up and down the river.

Wenamon prepared at once for his trip. Hrihor gave him only a small sum of gold and silver to pay for the wood. He had with him, also, his letters of introduction and an image of Amon, which would prove to all who saw it that he was on the business of the god.

On the sixteenth day of the eleventh month of the fifth year of the reign of Hrihor, he set obediently out for Tanis, the capital of the Delta. Here he delivered his letters to the prince, who received him kindly and managed to find a boat, commanded by a Syrian captain, which would carry the Egyptian across the Mediterranean to Byblos.

So Wenamon set out on his journey in a boat commanded by a man of another race and bearing with him a pitifully small sum of money and an image, to get wood for the great god of Egypt.

Do you remember the expedition that Hatshepsut sent forth to get myrrh-trees from the land of Punt? There were then five great ships, manned by Egyptian sailors, sent forth with rejoicing, received by natives of a strange country with courtesy and returning with untold wealth to their own country. Compare this expedition with Wenamon's disastrous trip on much the same mission, and you will realize how the position of Egypt in the world had changed.

Poor Wenamon! Hardly was the ship on which he sailed out of Tanis, when he discovered that in the excitement of sailing he had left behind him all his letters of introduction. Although he pleaded with the captain to turn back, the Syrian would not, but kept the boat headed for the sea. They put in for provisions at Dor. When the king of Dor heard that a messenger from the high priest of Amon had arrived in his harbor, he sent him a jar of wine, a joint of beef and several loaves of bread. Wenamon, glad to have a change from the food that the Syrian captain had provided, set himself down to a feast. When he had eaten all he wanted he returned to his cabin to rest, only to find that some villain had sneaked in there during his absence and stolen the jars of gold and silver from their hiding places. Wenamon was in despair. No money and no letters! What chance had he of getting the precious cedar wood?

Next morning early he went straight to the king of Dor.

"O King!" he cried, "I have been robbed in thy harbor. Since thou art the ruler of the land thou knowest all things and shouldst have my gold and silver restored to me."

"What is this which thou sayest?" the King replied. "If the thief who went on board thy ship and stole thy treasure belonged to my land, I would repay it to thee from my treasury. But the thief who robbed thee belongs to thine own ship. Yet tarry a few days and I will seek him."

So Wenamon waited for nine restless and despairing days. Then realizing that the king meant to do nothing for him, he set sail for Byblos. And the nearer he came to the land of the cedar trees the more worried he became about his lack of money. Once again the ship put into shore for provisions, this time at Tyre. While walking about the city Wenamon saw a party of men from Dor, who had come to do business in Tyre and carried with them a bag of silver. Wenamon and his friends set upon the men, grabbed the silver and ran for the boat. As they sailed out of the harbor, followed by the cries of the men, Wenamon shouted back, "Men of thy city robbed me of all my wealth. When it is returned to me I will give thee thine."

On up the coast sailed the Syrian captain and, four months and twelve days after leaving Thebes, Wenamon came to Byblos. He sent word at once requesting an audience with Zakar-Baal, the King. But the King refused to see him. Who was this man from Egypt who came without gifts or letters, and who arrived on a common merchant ship? Surely he was a man of no importance.

Wenamon waited patiently in Byblos. For twenty-nine days the harbor master came to him each morning, telling him that Zakar-Baal sent only one message. "Get thyself out of my harbor." Seeing that Wenamon paid no heed to the King's message the master ceased his daily visit. Still Wenamon did not go. Five months were passed in waiting. Finally Wenamon gave up in despair. Hearing that there

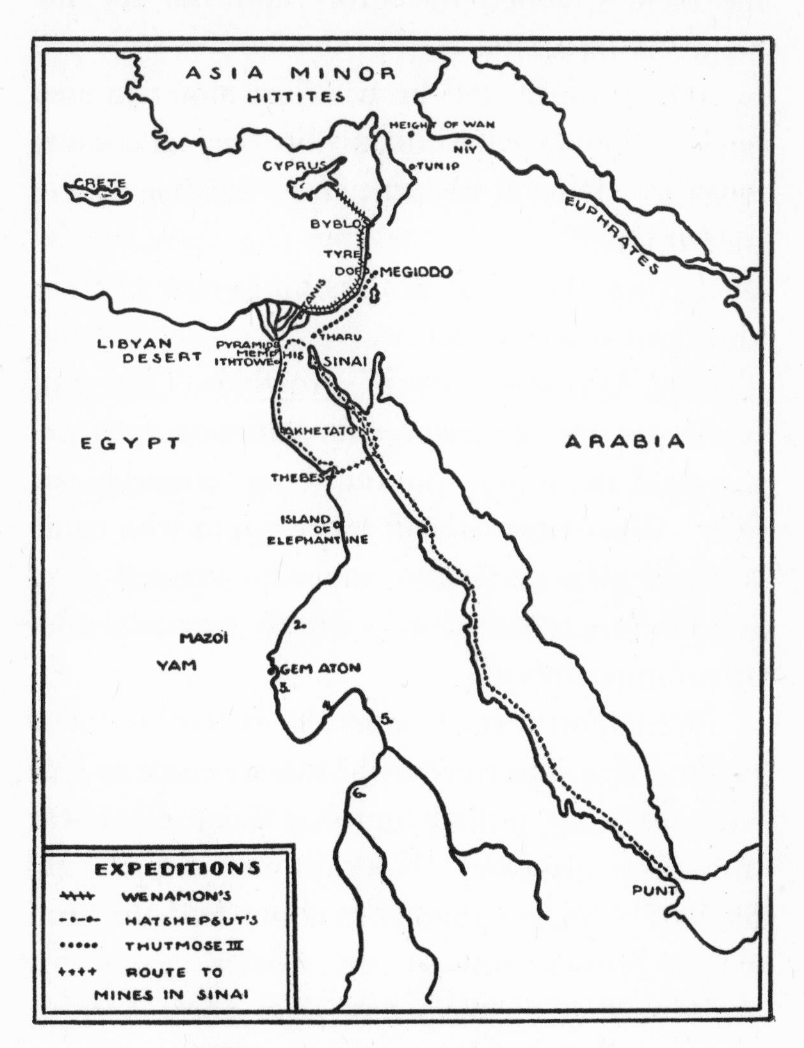

EGYPT AND THE ANCIENT WORLD

was a ship about to sail for Egypt he decided to take passage on it.

It was night and he was just about to step on the boat, when suddenly in the darkness a hand was laid on his arm and the voice of the harbor master spoke, telling him that Zakar-Baal had at last changed his mind and sent for him.

"What is this about?" growled Wenamon. "Art not thou the same man who hast told me day after day, 'Get thee out?' Dost thou wish that this ship should sail away without me and that I should be left forever in this land?" But though he grumbled he prepared for an audience with the King.

Next morning he was led to the fortress where Zakar-Baal awaited him. There sat the King in an upper chamber, leaning his back against the window. Behind him the waves of the Syrian Sea beat on the shore and the sun sparkled on the water.

"On what business hast thou come here?" asked the King, as Wenamon bowed low before him.

"I have come after the cedar-wood for the great barge of Amon, the king of the gods. Thy father gave wood for a barge like this, thy grandfather gave it, and thou must do likewise for the great god Amon, who watches over thy land as well as over Egypt," replied Wenamon.

"They did that truly, and if thou wilt give me something in return, I too will do it. Thy Pharaoh sent six laden ships in payment for the last wood which was taken," answered the King.

Angered at last by Wenamon's insistence that he give the cedar, he went on to say that he, Zakar-Baal, King of Byblos, was not the servant of any man in Egypt. He admitted to Wenamon that the god Amon watched over all the lands and had first watched over Egypt. But he could not understand how a country that had been the most learned in the world and the most powerful, could send out a messenger so pitifully equipped.

When the King had finished speaking Wenamon rose in anger and, holding up the image of Amon before Zakar-Baal, he said, "It is no miserable journey on which I have come. I am here only to claim that which Amon owns, for the trees, the ships upon the river, the sea itself are all his. And behold! Thou hast let this great god wait for thee all this time since he landed in thy harbor. Certainly thou didst know that he was here. It is true that the former kings sent silver and gold. But Amon gives something more valuable still, for Amon is the lord of life and health. If thou sayest to him, 'I will do it! I will do it!' and thou doest his commands, thou shalt live long, thou shalt be healthy, thou shalt be prosperous and thou shalt be pleasing to the whole land and to thy people. Is not this more than gold and silver?"

Wenamon's words were wasted. The King preferred money in his hand to promises for the future and would deliver no timber without payment. So Wenamon summoned a scribe and sent off a message to the King of Tanis. He asked him to send at once five gold vases and five of silver, five hundred rolls of papyrus, ten garments of royal linen, five hundred coils

A TRADER FROM THE ISLAND OF CRETE BRINGS GIFTS TO THE PHARAOH

of rope, twenty measures of lentils, and thirty measures of fish.

Many days passed before the messenger returned bringing in his care those things that Wenamon had requested. The King of Byblos, seeing that he was really to be paid, set three hundred men and three hundred oxen to cutting and hauling the cedar logs. Finally the work was done and Wenamon walked along the shore, rejoicing that his mission was accomplished and that he would soon be at sea, bearing home those logs he had been sent to fetch. He raised his eyes to look at the water over which he was so soon to travel. At that moment into the harbor sailed eleven ships—all bearing men from Dor, sent out to capture that man who had stolen a bag of silver from their countrymen in Tyre.

"Arrest him!" cried a man from one of the ships, when he recognized Wenamon. "Let not a ship of his pass to Egypt."

Once more had misfortune overtaken poor Wenamon. He fell on the sand in despair, weeping. When news of his plight was carried to Zakar-Baal, the King took pity on him. Perhaps he understood that Wenamon had tried to be a faithful servant and had used all the means at his command to carry out the orders of his ruler. At any rate he sent words of encouragement to cheer him and food and wine to comfort him.

The next morning the men of Dor demanded of the King of Byblos that Wenamon should be turned over to them. Zakar-Baal replied, "It is not right that I should arrest a messenger of Amon in my land. No—let him leave the harbor and once he has passed the entrance thou mayest catch him if thou canst."

So Wenamon set sail with his precious cedar, while the men of Dor waited only for him to clear the harbor before beginning the chase. Suddenly at he turned into the open sea a terrible tempest arose. The pursuing ships put back in all haste, but Wenamon had no choice but to sail on. And his boat, tossed by the waves, blown by the gale, was carried far out of her course and flung up on the coast of Cyprus.

When the people of Cyprus found the strange ship on their beach, they were greatly excited and determined to kill Wenamon and the men of his crew. But the Egyptian insisted that he be taken before the queen of the island.

They met the Queen walking in the streets, surrounded by her attendants. Wenamon, thrust forward by his captors, addressed the Queen in his own tongue. She could not understand him. Turning to the crowd who pushed up behind him he cried, "Is there none here who can speak with the tongue of Egypt?" One of the men of Cyprus stepped forward and, answering in Egyptian, he agreed to act as interpreter.

"Say to your Queen," said Wenamon, "that everywhere, even as far as Thebes, I have heard it said that though injustice may be done in every city, yet there is justice always done here. Say to her that I find that this is not so."

"What is this?" said the Queen. "Make thy meaning clear."

"Is it just," said Wenamon, "that when the wind and waves cast me all unwilling upon thy shore, thy men should set upon me to slay me? I am a messenger of Amon. If I do not return to my city they will seek me unceasingly. And these men of my crew are from Byblos. If thou permittest them to be slain, their lord will surely take ten crews of thine and slay them in payment."

When these words had been translated for the Queen, she ordered that Wenamon and his crew be released at once.

Here the story of Wenamon ends, for the papyrus on which he wrote it was partly burned, and we shall never know how he reached Egypt.

A SACRED BARGE LIKE THAT FOR WHICH WENAMON PROCURED THE CEDAR

XX

OLD EGYPT IS DEAD

(Time, About 1100–609 B.C.)

On Wenamon's return to Egypt he found the country no better off than he had left her. Hard times had come to stay. For many long unhappy years the land, that had been the most powerful in the world, was ruled by kings from foreign countries. First came the Libyans, who at last gained possession of the Delta by the simple process of moving in and gradually settling their families. The Egyptian army was filled with Libyan soldiers, and one of the more ambitious finally succeeded in proclaiming himself Pharaoh.

Then the Nubians, those dark-skinned, black-haired people from the south, took the country from the Libyans, and for more than thirty years the proud Egyptians were subject to that race.

It was the people from the northeast, those men who had settled in the Hittite country and who had once, years ago, tried to invade Egypt, who beat back the Nubians and took their turn ruling the unhappy dwellers on the Nile.

But Egypt was to rally once more. There is an old folk-tale of this time, in which the following story is told.

The country was divided among twelve friendly princes who ruled together peacefully. All twelve met together on one occasion to celebrate a religious holiday. On the last day of the celebration the princes met in the temple and the High Priest brought to them the golden goblets from which they were to pour wine on the ground as an offering to the gods. Through some mistake he brought only eleven goblets.

The last prince in line, Psamtik by name, seeing that there was no goblet for him, took his bronze helmet from his head and held it out to

THE PHARAOH GOES BEFORE HIS PEOPLE
His fan-bearers walk before him

receive the wine. Then suddenly all remembered how an oracle had once declared that the one of the twelve kings who poured an offering from a vessel of bronze should one day be king of all Egypt. Immediately the other kings turned on Psamtik and banished him to the swamps of the Delta. While he wandered among the swamps another oracle spoke to him. It told him that men of bronze would appear from the sea, who would help him punish those kings who had banished him. Men in bronze armor did indeed appear, having been forced by a tempest to land on the shores of the Delta. Psamtik engaged them to fight for him, succeeded in defeating the eleven kings, and proclaimed himself king of Egypt.

We do not know how much of this tale is true. We do know, however, that under the Pharaoh, Psamtik, Egypt was once more united and again became powerful and prosperous. It remained so all through his reign. But it was no longer a country of people who looked forward to fresh successes and new glories. Rather did they look backward into the past.

You have heard older people, remembering things that are gone say sadly, "Ah, those were the good old days!" So now did the Egyptians sigh for the past. It is hard for us, whose country is not yet three hundred years old, to realize that the Egyptians could look back over nearly three thousand years of their history. They remembered the stories of twenty-five hundred years earlier, when Imhotep was the wise man in Zoser's court and they made him a god. They talked of the time of Khufu when many men had labored, building the Great Pyramid, and they set to work to repair the pyramids. They thought of Uni, who made the first canals on the upper Nile; and they told their children stories of Harkhuf's triumphal procession through the land of the black men. They spoke with pride of Sekenere, killed at the head of his troops in the fight that brought Egypt back under Egyptian rule. And surely they remembered Sesostris, that wise king who had spent so much time and thought in making life easier and more comfortable for his people; and Thutmose, who led the armies of Egypt so far into Syria; and Rameses, who fought so bravely at Kadesh.

They restored old temples; they sought out the records and writings of the past and rearranged them. They revived old names and customs. They tried to imitate the old style of writing, although only the most learned could read the old hieroglyphs. But they could not bring back the old spirit of the land. And, perhaps because they looked backward rather than forward, after the death of Psamtik the country became the prey of whatever peoples wanted her. Syrians, Persians, Greeks, and at last Romans, had their turn.

Old Egypt—that country where men first learned to irrigate their lands, to live together in cities, to make things of copper; where they invented writing and an alphabet, made the first calendar and shadow-clock, erected monuments that thousands of years later stand as the proof of their skill; Old Egypt—the land of the first great explorers, traders, architects, artists, sculptors and craftsmen; Old Egypt—the light of knowledge for the whole ancient world—was dead.

But she lives again for those who want to find her. Perhaps you will read of her in books, in records, or in the letters that have been translated by those who have spent many patient years learning to read the old language. Perhaps, if you are very lucky, you will some day walk beside the Nile and see the Pyramids, the Sphinx, and the ruins of lordly temples; or you may even dig in the sands of the New Egypt for some of the lost treasures of the Old. Surely you will go to the museums to see those things that have been unearthed and preserved. There will be some things that you may be allowed to touch, and you can say to yourselves, "My hand is now resting on something that was made and loved by a man who belonged to one of the oldest and greatest countries in the history of the world. Yet though he lived so long ago, in a strange and distant land, he and his country-men were very like the people among whom I live today."

ACKNOWLEDGMENTS

I would like to express my indebtedness to the late Professor James Henry Breasted and to his publishers, The University of Chicago Press, for their permission to quote from the "Ancient Records" of Egypt, in translations of messages and letters.

I am indebted also to Methuen and Company, Ltd., of London, for permission to quote the "Song of the Shepherds," the "Song of the Threshers," and part of the "Exhortations and Warning to a School Boy," from the "Literature of the Ancient Egyptians," by Adolf Erman, translated by Aylward Blackman.

Thanks are due to Dr. H. E. Winlock, Curator of the Department of Egyptology of the Metropolitan Museum of Art in the city of New York, for permission to redraw photographs from the Museum collection; and to

Col. Sir H. G. Lyons, Director of the Science Museum, South Kensington, London, for permission to use the photograph, "Transport in Ancient Egypt."

To Dr. Reisner, Curator of the Department of Egyptian Art in the Museum of Fine Arts in Boston, I am indebted for permission to retell the story of the robbery of the tomb of Queen Hetep-heres; and to Dows Dunham, Associate Curator of the same Department, for his criticism of the story.

My thanks are due especially to Mr. Alan W. Shorter, Curator of the Department of Egyptian and Assyrian Antiquities of the British Museum in London, for his many kindly and helpful suggestions as to sources of material; and to his publishers—Sampson, Low, Marston and Company, Ltd.—as well as to him, for permission to use the plate illustrating Egyptian Hieroglyphic Writing, taken from his book, "Everyday Life in Ancient Egypt."

I am indebted also to the late Sir E. A. Wallis Budge and to his publishers—Kegan Paul, Trench, Trubner and Company, Ltd.—of London, for permission to quote from his book, "Legends of the Gods."

The illustrations of the book have all been taken from Egyptian material, usually as direct copies though in a few instances there have been adaptations, or composite arrangements from several sources. An attempt has been made to have all pictures and decorations correspond accurately in period to the text. In a few places such as chapters XI and XX this was not practical and exceptions have been made.

Through the painstaking cooperation of the Egyptian department of the Boston Museum of Fine Arts the drawings are more nearly authentic than would otherwise have been possible. Miss Elizabeth Eaton of the staff has given very great assistance in going over quantities of material and in helping to select what was most suitable. In addition to this Miss Lois Lord and Miss Virginia Field have had a large share both in research and in carrying out the actual drawings.

E. L. M.

INDEX